THE ELEGANT ONION

The Art of Allium Cookery

To my beloved Charlie,
who makes everything possible

Betty Cavage

A Garden Way Publishing Book

STOREY

Storey Communications, Inc.
Pownal, Vermont 05261

*Too often the poet sees but the tears that
live in an onion, not the smiles.*
—Anonymous

Cover art: Onions *by Pierre Auguste Renoir. Sterling and
Francine Clark Art Institute, Williamstown, Massachusetts.
Used by permission.*
Cover & Text Design: Cindy McFarland

Printed in the United States by Capital City Press
Second printing, October 1988

Library of Congress Cataloging-in-Publication Data

Cavage, Betty.
    The elegant onion.

    "A Garden Way Publishing book."
    Includes index.
    1. Cookery (Onions)   2. Onions.   I. Title.
TX803.05C38   1987   641.6′526   87-45011
ISBN 0-88266-460-3 (pbk.)
ISBN 0-88266-482-4 (h.c.)

Life itself is like an onion; it has a bewildering number of layers. You peel them off, one by one, and sometimes you cry.
—Carl Sandburg

TABLE OF CONTENTS

INTRODUCTION
1

APPETIZERS
28

SALADS AND DRESSINGS
42

SOUPS AND STEWS
54

ONIONS ALONE
74

ONIONS & FRIENDS
83

ENTRÉES
95

BREADS & PASTRIES
114

CONDIMENTS
129

SAUCES & SEASONINGS
142

INDEX
152

INTRODUCTION

D ISCOVER THE WONDERFUL WORLD OF ONIONS, and cooking need never be monotonous again.

Polite society no longer frowns on the onion and its family members—leeks, scallions, shallots, chives, and garlic. They occupy a place of honor in the cuisine of every country and appear with frequency and aplomb on menus around the globe. Everyone, from simple country peasants to the bluebloods of royalty, consumes them with gusto. Creative cooks everywhere revere their value and versatility. Gourmet chefs reach for them as automatically as they reach for their favorite kitchen tools. Imagine, for a moment, onionless cooking: vichyssoise without leeks, stew without onions, Béarnaise sauce without shallots, salads or dressings without scallions, spaghetti sauce without garlic, garnishing without chives—a sad state of affairs!

Rare is the cook who overlooks the come-hither appeal of creamy onion slices sizzled to perfection in a skillet, the fragrant goodness of onion soup simmered long and slowly on the back burner, or the satisfying crunchiness of onion rings piled high on a salad bowl of garden fresh greens. But there is much more to cooking with the onion family. Once you discover the versatility of these lusty aromatics, food preparation takes on a new dimension. Entrées come alive with texture, flavor, and color. Humdrum meals are transformed into gourmet delights.

This is a book written to help you discover, understand, and enjoy cooking with the onion family—without tears. Onion lovers will need no encouragement to tackle the recipes in this book. Our hope is to motivate the skeptical and coax the timid into

Let onion atoms lurk within the bowl And, scarce suspected, animate the whole.
—Sydney Smith

the piquant and pungent world of onions.

My first recollection of onions spans half a century to when I was a child growing up in England. Each spring we made our Easter pilgrimage to the hen house to gather a basket of large eggs for coloring. Painstakingly we wrapped each one in layers of tawny, papery-thin onion skins and tied them in place with yards of white thread. I still recall how we watched with eager anticipation as they bubbled in a large, cast-iron pot on the stove. As soon as the moment of doneness arrived, we spooned each egg carefully onto the fireplace hearth to drain and dry.

Next came the miracle—that wondrous moment when, threads snipped and onion skins peeled away, the eggs emerged in all their onion-tinted splendor. Each one was unique, beautifully decorated in variegated hues of burnished bronze, gold, sienna, and yellow. They disappeared without a trace that night, only to reappear on Easter morning hidden in nooks and crannies throughout the old house.

We lived in Cumberland, a picturesque county on the Scottish border, framed on one side by the Firth of Solway and the heathered hills of Scotland and on the other by the snow-capped mountains of the Lake District. Centuries before, invading Roman conquerors had built a winding fieldstone wall stretching from coast to coast. Sections of its crumbling remains meandered through our property. Wild chives and leeks grew among the tumbled rocks, where they blossomed in a glorious profusion of purple each spring.

Our house and garden rested on the site of an ancient Roman camp, where the rocky soil yielded old coins and artifacts along with an endless bounty of nature's treasures. Potatoes, turnips, cabbages, parsnips, carrots, scallions, leeks, and onions provided staples for the wholesome, rib-sticking meals that generated daily energy for the demands of country living.

During these formative years, cooking from scratch took on

MY ONION ROOTS

meaning and substance. Food preparation was never relegated to a necessity; it was always a joyous undertaking.

Each spring we were sent out with a large sack in search of wild greens for Granny's onion and nettle pudding. The recipe, an heirloom from generations past, was thought to cleanse and purify the blood at one sitting.

Led by Tom, our gardener, we searched out young dandelion leaves, wild winter cress, shepherd's purse, sheep sorrel, spiderwort, and the infamous nettle with its sharp sting.

Back in the pantry, the mixture was sorted, trimmed, and washed. After a brief steaming, it was chopped into a pan of boiled, diced onions and flavored with molasses and vinegar. As generous portions were doled out, we were cheerfully admonished to clean our plates. Nettle and onion pudding was required eating.

Granny lived on into her nineties and maintained that onions were one of the secrets of her longevity. She had an abiding passion for them, cooked and uncooked. Years later, when living in Bermuda, I often thought of Granny as I watched native islanders munch on onions in much the same way as they would apples. It is on this tiny pinpoint of land in the Atlantic where rich volcanic soil and a warm, subtropical climate combine to produce the most famous onion of all—the mild, sweet Bermuda. It is the island's most renowned resident and grows in onion patches from one end of this verdant paradise to the other.

Early settlers used the onion for food, either fresh or dried, but they also treasured it as a thirst preventive on an island where the only drinking water available was, and still is, rain.

The Bermuda onion, after embarking on its odyssey into the kitchens of the world, quickly became a culinary celebrity. Requests for the mild, sweet allium poured in from both continents and before long, the island was dubbed, "The Onion Patch." Even today native Bermudians are still referred to as "Onions."

My choice of onion for salads is the sweet Bermuda (if you can find it) or Spanish. Nothing matches their mild flavor and crisp texture. For a vivid color contrast, I slice or chop the red Italian onion into the fixings. If you don't have a sweet onion on hand, take the bite out of a cooking onion by soaking the slices in cold milk for 20 minutes. Or blanch them in boiling water for 10 minutes, drain, and crisp in ice water. Pat dry and use immediately.

Bermudians today staunchly maintain that no other onion in the world compares to theirs for sweetness, mildness, texture, and flavor. I am in complete agreement.

The most famous soup du jour of all times—onion—appears by popular demand everywhere in Bermuda, from the modest cedar kitchens of native islanders to the posh dining rooms of the magnificent hotels. Seasoned Bermudian cooks, many of whom claim they were weaned on its savory goodness, insist onion soup tastes even better served the second time around, after it mellows, and approaches pure perfection.

Bermuda is where the idea for this book germinated and inspiration welled to overflowing. Many of the recipes are Bermudian in charm and spirit, while others reflect the home-style cooking recalled from childhood. Besides their nostalgic value, each recipe is delicious in its own right and still in keeping with today's cooking.

Without exception, each presentation is dependent upon the involvement of the incredible onion family. Their unfailing support transformed this book from an idea into reality. What other residents of the garden patch can be converted into appetizers, soups, sandwiches, salads and dressings, side dishes, breads and pastries, entrées, sauces, gravies, condiments, and a dessert without being repetitious?

Onions, my dear readers, are nothing to sniff at!

ONIONS FOR HEALTH

Members of the onion family have been around for over five thousand years, providing people with an important staple in their diet. What most folks don't realize is that onions have been promoting good health at the same time. For the most part, the nutritional value of onions, leeks, scallions, shallots, chives, and garlic has been overlooked. Alliums are a storehouse of valuable nutrients, and their year-round availability makes them an indispensable tool in helping us to stay healthy.

Onions are a source of vitamins A and C, along with thiamine, riboflavin, and niacin. One medium-sized onion contains as much vitamin C as two apples, one banana, one tomato, or one orange. One cup of chopped, raw onions delivers 267 milligrams of potassium, 61 milligrams of phosphorus, and 46 milligrams of calcium. All are minerals essential to the normal structure and functioning of the body.

Over five thousand years ago, an account of onions and garlic as staples in the Sumerian diet appeared in our first written language, Sanskrit. Members of the onion family were chronicled in the oldest of written documents, the Tablets of Babylon and Assyria and in ancient Chinese scrolls, dating back over three thousand years. History tells us that these lusty aromatics were assigned to the highest strata in the majestic Hanging Gardens of Babylon.

NUTRITIVE VALUE OF 1 CUP OF CHOPPED, RAW ONIONS*

Water	89.0 percent
Calories	65.0
Protein	3.0 grams
Fat	trace
Carbohydrates	15.0 grams
Calcium	46.0 milligrams
Phosphorus	61.0 milligrams
Iron	.9 milligram
Sodium	15.0 milligrams
Potassium	267.0 milligrams
Vitamin A	trace
Vitamin B	.05 milligram
Thiamin	.05 milligram
Riboflavin	.07 milligram
Niacin	.3 milligram
Vitamin C (Ascorbic Acid)	1.0 milligram

*Source: USDA Home and Garden Bulletin, *Nutritive Value of American Foods*

The Israelites, during their forty years of wandering in the Sinai Desert, complained bitterly to Moses of their need and longing for onions and garlic, a staple in their diet before the parting of the Red Sea and their exodus from Egypt.

When you eat onions, you are consuming fiber, or roughage, a natural laxative that creates bulk in the intestinal tract by its ability to absorb water like a sponge. Dietary fiber is important to good health and also helps you to lose weight. Fiber cuts down on fat absorption during digestion. Bulking up with high fiber foods such as onions, leeks, and scallions makes you feel fuller and eat less. Dieters can rest easy in the knowledge that one medium-sized onion contains only thirty-eight calories. Live a better-regulated, healthier life. Put some alliums in it.

ONIONS IN MEDICINE

Norman conquerors slung sacks of *oignons* over their shoulders when they waded ashore on English beaches during William's invasion in 1066 A.D. Britons, quick to appreciate the value of this new-found edible delight, proceeded to plant, propagate, and anglicize it.

Throughout history true believers have maintained steadfastly that onions and garlic keep the body healthy. As early as 3000 B.C., healers and physicians in the Far East advocated eating them for everything from infections to hypertension. Hippocrates, one of the world's most famous healers, prescribed onions and garlic to heal wounds, fight pneumonia, and as a diuretic.

In 1596 a book entitled *The Great Herbal* claimed that onion juice had properties to grow hair on a bald head, cure fits, and remedy the bites of mad dogs. Onions were believed to aid digestion, clear bad complexions, banish arthritis, cleanse the blood, and cure the common cold.

During the plagues and epidemics of the eighteenth century, onion slices were spread about to act as traps for the causes of the diseases. During his trip to the Galapagos, Captain James Cook ordered his crew aboard H.M.S. *Beagle* to consume large amounts of onions in an effort to prevent scurvy.

Remember Grandmother's old-fashioned remedy for chest colds and respiratory ailments? Onions, chopped and boiled down to a mush, were sprinkled with camphorated oil and wrapped in flannel. Next, this steaming, fragrant poultice was applied to the patient's back or chest. Cough syrups of onion juice and honey appeared at the slightest cough or wheeze. Earaches meant roasted

American Indians held onions and garlic in great esteem, consuming them with regularity and brewing them in potions for medicinal cures. Cortez records eating garlic on his plunderous pilgrimage through Mexico. When Marquette and his men almost succumbed to starvation while exploring the Great Lakes, Indians saved their lives with presents of onions and garlic. Chicago is said to have derived its name from Marquette's campsite on Lake Huron, *Cigaga-Wunj,* an Indian name meaning "place of the wild garlic."

onions applied at regular intervals until the pain and infection subsided. Bee stings and burns were always on the receiving end of raw onion slices to relieve itching and pain. These homemade remedies still constitute health care in many parts of the world.

Today, medical research all over the world is investigating claims, once thought to be superstitions, that onion and garlic help prevent and cure major health problems. In many instances scientists have substantiated their findings and are starting to join the ranks of believers.

Garlic contains an ingredient named allicin, often called Russian penicillin, which has had widespread use and application in the USSR to combat infection. Many consider it to be the very first antibiotic. Russian scientists report that raw onion, chewed for five minutes, renders the lining of the mouth and throat completely sterile.

A wide variety of research continues to support the possibility that onions and garlic offer some protection against heart disease. Studies by a team of researchers at George Washington School of Medicine determined recently that onions and garlic both contain chemically similar compounds that inhibit blood clotting. Research conducted at East Texas State College confirms earlier suggestive findings that yellow onions contain a potent agent for lowering blood pressure called Prostaglandin A_1.

Separate studies conducted in India and reported in the Indian *Journal of Medicine* confirmed that onions have a cholesterol-lowering effect on the human body. Patients were monitored for the effects of eating a high-fat diet with and without the addition of onion supplements. Those fed ten grams of onion a day showed a marked decrease in cholesterol concentration in the blood.

A professor of medicine at Tufts University documented proof that onions raise the blood level of high-density lipoprotein, HDL, the "good cholesterol," believed to help clear the arteries of fatty deposits. HDL levels in the blood jumped as much as thirty percent after the juice of a single yellow or white onion was ingested. Research is now in progress to determine which ingredient in an onion triggers this positive HDL effect.

At the Anderson Hospital and Tumor Institute in Houston, preliminary research indicates that onion and garlic may prevent cancer in its initial stages. The sulfur in onion and garlic oils actually inhibits the growth of cancer in its "initiation stage," where interaction occurs with a normal cell. Eating more fiber-rich foods, such as onions, leeks, and scallions, may be of great importance in helping to avert colon cancer.

What of the onion and garlic preparations available in health food stores—Do they contain medical properties capable of effecting prevention and cures? The consensus is no. Manufacturing processes are quite harsh and destroy most of the anti-bacterial and anti-clotting properties.

THE ONION PATCH

A garden symbolizes many things—survival, relaxation, pride, a challenge, love. During the war years, we English tilled ours out of necessity and in hopes of making some small contribution on the home front. Now in our golden years, my husband and I garden for the sheer joy of it and the blessed reassurance of the grand design. Regardless of its purpose, a garden's message is profoundly simple. Life goes on.

We live in western New York on the Canadian border. Contrary to popular belief, it does not snow there all year round. Late thaws and early frosts make for tricky growing seasons, but each spring the sun warms, the rain falls, and our half acre of rich, black soil is reborn. A doubting Thomas has no place in our onion patch.

Through the years, we have grown everything from asparagus to zucchini. Only the onion patch is a constant. From spring's first harbinger, delicate emerald-green chives to sweet scallions,

LATIN NAMES

ONIONS *Allium cepa*
CHIVES *Allium schoenoprasum*
GARLIC *Allium sativum*
GARLIC CHIVES *Allium tuberosum*
LEEKS *Allium porrum*
SHALLOTS *Allium ascalonicum*
WELSH ONIONS *Allium fistulosum*

distinctive shallots, redolent leeks, hearty garlic, and aromatic onions, the allium family members are permanent residents.

Well before the predicted last spring frost date, we begin to plant onions. Cold temperatures do not hurt onions and a longer growing period produces plenty of verdant top growth. The more leaves an onion grows, the bigger the bulb it produces.

To grow onions it really doesn't matter whether you select seeds, "sets" (tiny onions which grow into big ones), or small onion transplants. It's a matter of preference and the growing season in the area where you live.

Onions grown from seed offer the widest choice of varieties, but patience must prevail. You will wait from 100 to 120 days for mature bulbs to develop from seed. Planting onion "sets" restricts your choice of selection, but green onion leaves will appear quickly and the bulbs mature three to four weeks earlier than those grown from seed. Purchasing small plants or transplants reduces the choice of varieties even more but allows you to produce an edible crop soonest.

Your local nursery or garden shop will recommend the best varieties for you to grow. Get a catalog from a reliable seed house if you want to start your onions from seed. It will tell you what varieties grow best where; the number of days from planting to maturity; the bulb's shape and flavor; whether it is suitable for eating raw, cooking, pickling, and/or storing; and which varieties are suitable for growing your own sets.

Our preference for growing onions is sets. We select Ebenezer or Stuttgarten varieties, and our strategy is to plant them two or three inches from each other in all directions. We call it our "rubbing elbows" technique. Don't be afraid to crowd your onions when you plant. If your garden plot is limited in size, plant the sets as close as one inch apart. You can still realize good results.

The onion family thrives in a well-worked, friable soil that is weed free. Compatible as alliums are, they do not tolerate weeds very well.

Mother Nature smiles on the onion patch. So take advantage of her benevolence and grow your own alliums. Collectively, they constitute the most important flavoring discovery ever made.

ONION FLOWERS

One of the most spectacular sights in the garden is the flowers of the giant onion plant (*Allium giganteum*). These magnificent specimens are ornamental alliums grown for display only.

Towering four feet above the ground, each stately stalk is topped by a massive, nine-inch globe of hundreds of tiny, lavender, honey-filled blossoms. Beloved of bees and garden enthusiasts alike, this dazzling summer delight lasts twenty-one days and can be used as a cut flower. When it is allowed to dry on the stalk, it becomes a fragile sunburst of topaz rosettes with black seed centers. Perfect for dry arrangements!

Onions can make even heirs and widows weep.
—Benjamin Franklin

SWEET ONIONS

Growing giant sweet onions is downright rewarding and lots of fun. What greater joy than a juicy cheeseburger piled high with crunchy sweet onion slices or a garden fresh salad topped with sweet onion rings?

For growing sweet onions, we select the White Sweet Spanish and the Bermuda White. Because both varieties require an early start and thrive in cool weather, we grow them from transplants as tall and as thick as a pencil. The more cool weather growth the plants receive, the larger the onions will be at harvest.

To ensure big onions, fertilize and water regularly. Begin fertilizing when the plants are six to eight inches high, then again in three to four weeks. Several more applications of fertilizer throughout the growing season will produce an onion crop you will boast about forever. Weed the patch regularly throughout the summer.

Harvest your onions when the tops lose their green color, turn brown, and begin to wither. Don't, whatever you do, allow the bulbs to stay in the ground once the tops are dead. Loosen the plants with a spading fork before pulling them out of the ground. Harvest your onion bounty on a warm, sunny day. Leave the onions bottom-side up in the garden for two or three days, until they are dry, and keep the roots away from the ground.

Once the tops are completely dry down to the neck of the bulb, cut the leaves off with shears. Make sure not to cut into the bulb or to cut the roots off.

Use a gentle touch when handling onions so as not to bruise or crack the dry outer layer of the onion bulbs. Damage encourages infection and rot.

Onions require a drying, or "curing," period of up to two weeks. I spread them out in a shady, warm place with lots of air circulation. Turn the bulb several times during drying to promote even curing. Sort the onions according to size and hang them in mesh bags or old panty hose. You can store them in slotted crates or place them in a single layer, necks down, on chicken netting suspended in a cold, dry location.

Use the thick-necked onions first, as they do not keep well. For permanent storage, move the onions into a dry, cool, frost-free and preferably dark storage place. The storage temperature for onions must not be above 45°F, 7°C, with a relative humidity of 60 to 70 percent.

CHIVES

With a minimum of effort, you can have a supply of chives year round. I keep a pot on my kitchen windowsill in the wintertime. In the spring, chives can be started from seeds indoors to plant in the garden for summer growth. Once the seeds germinate, move the plants to a cooler location. Replant when the seedlings are a few inches high in a rich, well-worked soil in the garden. Harvest chives when the green leaves are longer than three inches. Keep

---

ONION LOVER'S DELIGHT

Slice generous chunks of fresh, dark pumpernickel bread. Layer on hearty slabs of Liederkranz cheese with crunchy sweet onion rings. Slather with mustard to taste and wash down with steins of foaming beer. Not for the faint hearted!

them cut regularly throughout their growing season or the leaves will toughen. Cut about an inch above the white stems. Do not snip off the tips only.

SCALLIONS

A scallion is a very young onion pulled from the garden before it fully matures, while its top is tender and green. Early scallions do not form bulbs. When a small bulb forms, it can be used for pickling onions. The best-known onion variety to plant for scallions is White Lisbon.

SHALLOTS

No need to worry about finding the elusive shallot in supermarkets or paying the exorbitant price they command. You can grow enough shallots for year-round use. Shallot bulbs multiply in the garden. Their middle name is Productivity. Use sets and plant them further apart than onions, pointed ends up, to their full depth. Harvest the bulbs when the tops dry back. Pull them and dry them just like onions. Shallots have a longer staying life than onions, quite often up to ten or twelve months.

GARLIC

Growing garlic is simplicity itself. Break up a garlic bulb into cloves early in the spring when the soil is workable. Plant each clove separately, four inches apart and two inches deep. Harvest, dry, and store garlic in the same way as onions.

You can grow garlic chives by planting some extra cloves and harvesting the thin green stems. Don't use the garlic bulbs for cooking after you snip the stems. The flavor suffers.

Provence with her garlic-scented smile.
—Rudyard Kipling

LEEKS

Growing leeks is well worth the effort. Because leeks are a slow-growing crop, we start them indoors quite early and set them out in the garden later as transplants. We set them in the bottom of a narrow furrow four to six inches deep. As the plants grow, we gradually fill the furrow with soil and in this way keep the stems white. Blanching with soil is the secret of beautiful white stems. If you live in a climate where winter is not too severe, leave them in the ground and dig them as needed. They are at their best when they are young, tender, and freshly dug. This is the time we enjoy eating them raw. The first leeks are usually ready to harvest a few weeks before the first frost.

If your garden freezes hard and deep as ours does, dig out the leeks as late as is practical and store them in a cool, frost-free place in sand, or clean, slice, and blanch them for freezing. Leeks do not dry well.

LOW-SALT COOKING

Before delving too far into the book, you will notice a definite lack of specifics regarding the use of salt in recipes. There is a reason. For many years I have dedicated myself to the principles of low-salt cooking because of family blood pressure problems. I use no salt when I cook.

Today, hypertension poses a serious threat to our national health. Statistics indicate that one out of every five Americans suffers from high blood pressure. For those who have a tendency in that direction, salt can trigger high blood pressure. For those who already suffer from it, the use of salt can aggravate the condition seriously. Most people consume five to twenty-five times more salt than they require. We have become an oversalted society where everything from peanuts to porterhouse steaks is salted liberally without concern.

Do not think, for a moment, that the alternative to saltless cooking is bland, tasteless food. Absolutely not! Fragrant herbs, savory seasonings and spices, tangy lemon juice and fresh parsley join hands with aromatic onions, leeks, scallions, shallots, chives, and garlic to flavor foods with savoir faire. All are flavor makers in the truest sense of the word and my constant kitchen companions.

Put away the salt shaker when you cook. Or if you must, use it with discretion. You will feel better and live longer.

HERBS FOR ONIONS

Onions respond warmly to gourmet touches—a sprinkling of colorful paprika, freshly ground pepper, chopped fresh parsley, tangy grated cheese, or spicy nutmeg. Perk up your onion cooking with one or more of the following herbs and spices:

basil	turmeric
marjoram	caraway seeds
oregano	chili powder
sage	curry powder
thyme	dill
red pepper	

COOKING TIPS

Cooking successfully comes from doing the right thing at the right time in the right way. Good cooks are made not born.

For the most part, I rely on my kitchen knives to carry the work load. My preference is high-carbon steel knives with well-anchored blades that sharpen easily. Three favorites are never out of reach: a paring knife for trimming, paring, and cutting; a utility knife for slicing, cutting, and coring; and a chef's knife for chopping, cutting, and slicing.

My cutting board is made of polyethylene. It is large enough to give me lots of elbow room, cleans like magic, does not dull my knives, and is non-absorbent and much more sanitary than wood. It's an indispensable kitchen companion.

SAUTÉ SAVVY

To sauté onions, leeks, shallots, or garlic successfully, first heat the pan before adding the shortening. Use a combination of butter and oil, first for flavor and second to prevent scorching. Oil has a higher heating point than butter, so a combination works well.

Both the pan and the shortening must be hot enough to sear the food, seal in flavor, and prevent it from sticking. Keep the heat constant from the moment the cooking starts until the desired degree of doneness is reached.

Use a pan large enough to accommodate the food without crowding, so that steam does not form. Stir constantly and keep the pan in motion. Cook quickly over even heat until limp and translucent. DO NOT BROWN OR SCORCH. This will make the taste of onions, leeks, shallots, or garlic bitter.

You will find butter specified in most recipes because of my taste preference and because it contains the least additives. If preference decrees it or cholesterol poses a problem, substitute a light, polyunsaturated margarine.

I am no stranger to my food processor and blender. When manufacturers' directions are followed, they behave magnificently and save me countless hours of labor with a mere flick of the wrist.

To take the muss and fuss out of crushing garlic, I use a garlic press. This dandy little helpmate retains the pulp while pressing out the oil and garlic meat. Using a press makes for a stronger garlic flavor because the essential oils and juice are released. Mine has a hinged plunger that fits into the cylinder where the garlic cloves go and can be used to crush shallots and onions. Just remember to clean it immediately, before the pulp dries and plugs the holes.

Cooking becomes second nature as you get to know your pots and pans and rely on your own judgment to measure cooking times. At best, a recipe time is just a rule of thumb. I firmly believe in following instincts rather than a timer. After all, your own judgment is the best cook's tool that you can own.

And if the boy have not a woman's gift
To rain a shower of commanded tears,
An onion will do well for such a shift.
—William Shakespeare

ONIONS WITHOUT TEARS

Mine eyes smell onions. I shall weep anon.
—William Shakespeare

Only one member of the allium family, the onion, is capable of inducing tears. Leeks, scallions, shallots, chives, and garlic rarely, if ever, evoke this physical reaction. Crying results when the cut surface of the onion releases volatile sulfuric compounds into the air. Once the compounds vaporize, they irritate the eyes and bring on the tears.

If you tend to weep easily when peeling this lusty aromatic, there are different ways to overcome the problem. You might clip a clothespin on your nose, or try mind over matter. The youngest of my sons generously proffered his scuba mask and tank. In deference to Jacques Cousteau and his lofty principles, I declined the offer. There are moments during my chopping frenzies, however, when I am tempted to reconsider.

TO FREEZE AN ONION

Select top-quality, fully mature onions for freezing. Do not attempt to freeze whole onions. The results will disappoint you. Peel the onion, slice or chop it, and store the desired amounts in freezer bags with a twist tie. Freeze and dispense the amounts as needed for cooking.

Keep in mind that frozen onions do not retain their crispness when thawed, so don't try to use them raw in salads or as garnishes.

Do not store frozen onions any longer than three months.

To shed fewer tears when peeling onions, try the following:

- Refrigerate the onion first. The coldness retards the vaporization process.

- Slice off the stem end but leave the root end intact. The cells that cause the irritation are concentrated at the base of the onion. Trim this off at the last possible moment.

- Peel under cold, running water.

- Rinse your hands often while chopping or slicing.

- Chew on a crust of bread.

- Keep your mouth tightly closed while peeling.

- Place the cut side of the onion face down on the chopping board while slicing or dicing.

- Place the onion in boiling water for thirty seconds to loosen the skin. Remove and drain. Cool, trim off the top and tail. Slip off the skin.

If tears appear when all else fails, I usually grin and bear it. A few tears are a small price to pay for the infinite ways in which onions enrich our cooking.

SOME ONION FACTS

Did you know that the Seven of Spades, a gardener for the Queen of Hearts in *Alice's Adventures in Wonderland*, was ordered beheaded for bringing the cook tulip bulbs instead of onions? Perhaps his chances of remaining in one piece would have been greater if he had presented the cook with lily bulbs. Onions, believe it or not, are members of the elegant lily family known botanically as alliums.

Over four thousand years ago the onion symbolized the universe to Egyptians and was worshipped as a god. Herodotus, a Greek historian of the fifth century B.C., chronicled the astronomical amounts of money paid for the onions and garlic eaten by the slaves during the construction of the Great Pyramid, in what was probably the first cost accounting of a food budget in history. It was during the building of the Pyramid of Cheops that the first organized labor strike occurred, when the slaves, en masse, sat down and refused to work until they were guaranteed their daily rations of garlic and onions.

When we eat an onion, we are ingesting an *Allium cepa*—one of our oldest cultivated foods. As it grows, the onion forms a succulent, aromatic bulb at its base, whose crisp, snow white flesh is edible, as are its long, hollow leaves better known to us as scallions. A hollow flower stalk, taller than the leaves, blossoms each spring into clusters of beautiful white and purple flowers.

◇　◇　◇

Onions are considered true bulbs. This means that they store enough nourishment to provide food for the leaves and blossoms throughout the blooming period. That's why an onion doesn't need sun to sprout, as evidenced by those tiny green shoots we sometimes find growing from the top.

◇　◇　◇

Each onion is a sphere of thin, fleshy layers folded over each other and wrapped tightly around the bud. In onion circles these are called scales. To hold the onion together, Mother Nature provides a disc or hardened stem tissue called a basal plate.

◇　◇　◇

A dry onion is one that has been allowed to ripen in the sun after harvesting. This is called curing. During this period, the onion develops a dry, papery-thin skin known as a tunic, which protects the flesh during storage. Once they are cured, onions are available year round.

◇　◇　◇

Growers produce some fifteen million bushels of onions annually, ranking them fourth among commercial vegetable crops in the United States. Peak production is in Texas and California. Imports from around the world make a variety of onions available throughout the year.

◇　◇　◇

Like other garden patch residents, onions grow in a fascinating array of colors, shapes, and sizes. Onion skins vary from silvery white through pale yellow to dark brown and purple or red. Shapes range from round or global to a flattened global and oval. Sizewise, onions run the gamut from the huge Spanish, often weighing in at half a pound and measuring five inches in diameter, to the diminutive silver-skinned pearl at one-half inch around.

◇   ◇   ◇

An onion's sweetness, blandness, or pungency is determined by soil and climate. A reliable rule of thumb: the warmer the climate, the milder the onion. Don't expect to judge an onion's pungency by its color, although shape and size might provide some clues. Look for a flat or round onion, three inches or larger, to be sweeter and milder.

◇   ◇   ◇

Some of the more popular dry onions are classified as follows:

BERMUDA ONIONS—Meet the mildest and sweetest member of the onion gang. At one time it was grown exclusively on the island of Bermuda; now it is simulated in different areas of the United States, but it is still difficult to find in this country.

Crisp, delicately flavored, and juicy, with sweet, snow-white flesh, the Bermuda is eaten raw or cooked. Its storage life is shorter than other onions, and it is at its best when used immediately after harvesting in spring.

Flattened global in shape, Bermuda onions grow to one and a half to four inches. Its color varies from white to tan, sometimes red, with a yield of two or three to a pound.

SPANISH ONIONS—Sometimes called the Valencia, this onion is classified as sweet. Its flesh is milky, crisp, juicy, and not as sweet as the Bermuda. It can be eaten raw or cooked. It is not an exceptionally hardy onion, but it keeps longer than the Bermuda. Global in shape, Spanish onions grow from three to five inches in diameter and can weigh up to half a pound apiece. They vary in color from light yellow to fawn.

AROUND THE WORLD WITH ONIONS

English	Onion
Welsh	Gibbon
French	Oignon
Spanish	Cebolla
German	Zweibel
Italian	Cipolla
Greek	Krommuon
Chinese	Yang-ts'ung
Japanese	Tamanegi
Portuguese	Cebola
Russian	Luk
Swahili	Kitunguu
Indian	Piyaz
Yiddish	Tsibele
Swedish	Rödlök
Dutch	Ui

Onions always travel with armies. Initially, it was on the belief that they made soldiers valiant. When defeats dispelled this myth, the onion retained its place among the ranks to enliven the dullness of army food.

RED ITALIAN, OR CREOLE ONIONS—Mild enough to eat raw, this onion is stronger in flavor than the Bermuda or Spanish. Its crisp, variegated flesh does not lend itself to cooking as it becomes watery and the color runs. Red onions are global in shape and covered with a red or purple skin. They are fairly hardy and yield three or four per pound. Use them in salads or for garnishing.

GLOBE, OR YELLOW ONIONS—The most widely used of all onions, these are the workhorses of the allium family. Globes are all-purpose onions with a strong, pungent flavor. Their size varies from one and a half to three inches. They are global in shape with pointed stem ends. Skins are usually yellow but can be white or red. Yellow onions have a hardy storage life and number three to five per pound.

WHITE ONIONS—These shimmery, small, silver-skinned onions are harvested before maturity and are known as boilers or picklers. Boilers measure from one to two inches in diameter. Global in shape, they are cooked whole. Picklers measure no more than 1 inch in diameter and are used in soups and stews and whole with other vegetables. Pearl onions less than 1 inch in diameter are cocktail onions, the kind you discover at the bottom of a dry martini. All are fairly strong in flavor.

WELSH ONION—Despite its name, this onion is not grown in Wales. Its name is a derivation of the German *welsche*, meaning "foreign," given to it when it was introduced into Europe toward the end of the Middle Ages. It is sometimes called the Japanese bunching onion. In China, Japan, and Britain, it is the principal home garden onion. Its bulb is elongated and only slightly swollen with hollow, cylindrical leaves. Cooks use it as a substitute for spring onions or for seasoning.

GOURMET ONIONS

VIDALIA SWEET—Tender, sweet, mild and succulent, the Vidalia is eaten like an apple in south Georgia where it's grown. Like the Walla Walla Sweets, these large, plump onions are harvested early, before they develop a strong flavor. Usually available in May and June, they perish rapidly and should be used immediately.

WALLA WALLA SWEET—Round, firm, succulent and flavorful, these onions are from Washington State and are winter hardy. They are juicy, mild, and crisp with pale flesh.

MAUI—Grown on a volcanic peak in the state of Hawaii, Maui onions are becoming famous among gourmets for their distinctive, appealing flavor.

TEXAS SWEETIES—One of the leading crops of Texas is onions, and these are the state's answer to gourmet onions from Vidalia, Walla Walla, and Maui. Texas Sweeties come in red, yellow, and white varieties.

> Zesty Mexican tacos, those palate-pleasing ambassadors from south of the border, combine distinctive packaging with a spectacular combination of ingredients. Finely chopped onion tops the list.

SHOPPING FOR ONIONS

Shop selectively when buying onions. The tendency is to purchase the handiest of whatever the local grocery store carries. Please don't! Each variety of onion is a specialist in its own right, and the difference comes through in a recipe. There's no need to settle for yellow cooking onions all the time. Let your grocer know what you are looking for.

Top quality onions are easy to spot. Look for bright, dry, crackly skins that glisten. Select firm, symmetrical onions with thin necks and without blemishes. Avoid, at all costs, onions with a spongy feel and soft necks. Mold or moisture around the base or neck indicates decay. Onions with soft discolorations are rotting. Green shoots sprouting out of the top signal poor texture and flavor. Reject any onions with a wilted, weathered, or leathery look.

Store onions properly, and your rewards will be long lasting. Good circulation of air is essential. The more air that circulates around each bulb, the less chance of spoilage. Store onions in a dark, dry place at about 50°F. Direct light stimulates the production of chlorophyll, which turns an onion's flesh green and its flavor bitter. Do not refrigerate onions. Damp air encourages mildew and rot.

An old pair of panty hose is the perfect vehicle for storing onions. Hang a pair securely in the storage area. Slip an onion down inside the leg and make a knot. Add another onion, make another knot. Continue adding and knotting until each leg is filled. When you need an onion, snip below the knot, starting at the foot and working up. Sheer elegance!

If you're blessed with a garden and an onion crop, leave the long stems intact after curing and braid a series of bulbs together. Hang these ropes of onions from hooks in a cool, dry storage area.

When shopping, I give a wide berth to the ever-increasing array of convenience onion products on the shelves. This includes onion and garlic powders, onion and garlic juices, dehydrated onion flakes, onion and garlic salts, and freeze-dried soup mixes. Besides being oversalted, they tend to become rancid and stale very quickly. Up front they may save some time and a few tears, but at no time will they compare to the real thing. Cross them off your shopping list.

> From hamburgers, the all-American favorite, to watercress canapés, the diminutive darlings of the tea set, members of the onion family yield a wealth of support in transforming ordinary sandwich fare into taste-tempting delights. Like Wimpy of Popeye fame, I share a passion for cheeseburgers that transcends all else. Hot off the grill, oozing melted cheese, and topped with mounds of crisp sweet onion rings—they are unsurpassed.

SCALLIONS

Scallions are the mild-mannered member of the allium family. A very young onion pulled from the ground before it fully matures and while the top is still green is called a scallion. Scallions and green onions are one and the same.

Completely edible, from the green hollow leaves and white stalks to the tender small bulbs, scallions have a mild, sweet oniony flavor. The smaller the bulb, the milder the flavor. They are always sold fresh, usually in bunches of six to eight plants, with their bulbs and leaves intact.

The peak season for scallions is May through July, but they are available year round. Look for crisp green tops and firm white bulbs that are straight or slightly curved in shape. Fresh-appearing leaves indicate that they haven't advanced to the strong, stringy stage. Avoid any scallions with browned roots and wilted tops.

Scallions are perishable, so store them in the refrigerator, unwashed, in a perforated plastic bag for three to five days. Do not freeze, as the results will be disappointing.

To prepare, rinse well under cold running water after trimming the roots and removing any wilted tops. Cut off any coarse outer stem coverings. Pull off any damp, thin membranes covering the white stalk.

Scallions can be eaten whole as well as sliced, chopped, and minced. Use the leaves for soup flavoring. Only four calories per scallion places them high on a dieter's YES list. They make great flavorers in appetizers, dips, salads, dressings, and sauces.

LEEKS

Every family has a nonconformist. In the onion tribe, it is the leek. Without a doubt, it is the funniest looking and the dirtiest member of the household.

Unlike onions, leeks do not grow bulbs. Their thick white stalks are the same size as their roots, flaring into a series of broad, flat, green leaves almost ribbon-like in appearance. They are cold weather alliums, capable of tolerating warm temperatures. Mild and sweet, leeks lay claim to a distinctive flavor all their own. Leek lovers consider them to be the king of the soup onions.

Select flexible, fresh-looking leeks with tightly rolled bases and crisp green tops in a small- to medium-sized range. Avoid any with large bulbous ends, as they tend to be tough with a woody texture. Pass up those with limp, discolored tops.

Because they do not have a papery outer-skin protection like onions, leeks are perishable and require refrigeration. Store in a perforated plastic bag, unwashed, for three to five days. Leeks do

In Great Britain, Welsh warriors adorned their hat bands with leeks to distinguish themselves from the enemy during the confusion of battle. Today all good Welsh wear leeks, now the national emblem of Wales, on St. David's Day in commemoration of the Victory of King Cadwallader over the Saxons in 640 A.D.

not freeze well.

While growing, leeks are surrounded by tall mounds of dirt to keep them white. This tends to trap sand and grit inside as the plant develops. Leeks should be washed with determination and elbow grease to flush out the dirt between layers.

To prepare leeks, cut off the shaggy root hairs and remove any tough or damaged outer leaves. Using a sharp, pointed knife, pierce the leeks where the white part joins the green leaves. Slice lengthwise to within one half inch of the bottom in several places. Spread the base and leaves apart and wash well under cold running water. Cut off the soft tops, leaving one or two inches of tender greens. Save the tops for soup and stock.

Available year round and especially in the fall, leeks are not as easily come by as onions, but they are worth looking for. For the most part, they are served cooked and are marvelous in soups, stews, and quiches and braised in salads.

SHALLOTS

Shallots lend an air of aristocracy to the onion family. They are its most sophisticated member and the least known or understood except to gourmet cooks, who prize them for sauce making. In the sauces of French haute cuisine, where their distinctive flavor knows no peer, shallots are indispensable.

Like garlic, shallots grow in bulbs covered with a papery brown skin and filled with cloves. Their straight stems, pencil-like in appearance, cannot be eaten. Shallots have a tiny, spherical appearance and resemble small pointed onions. They come in three varieties: red, greenish white, and purple. They are available year round.

Shallots combine the aromatic characteristics of onion and garlic. Their distinctive flavor is less overpowering than either, with a delicacy that makes them ideal for sauces and epicurean cuisine.

Select small, firm, plump bulbs that are uniform in shape, with a dry, papery skin. Purchase only a few at a time, as shallots tend to dry up quickly. You may find them separated into cloves in the produce section of your grocery store. Reject any with green shoots, as sprouting destroys the flavor and texture.

Keep shallots in a cool, dark spot but do not refrigerate, as the damp air encourages rot. Direct light produces chlorophyll and makes for a bitter flavor.

To prepare, remove the top and tail of the shallot with a sharp knife. Peel by using your fingernails to pull off the skin and the first layer of flesh attached to it.

Shallots can be eaten raw or cooked. Use them whole, slivered, chopped, or minced. When sautéing, mince fine so as not to subject them to too much heat. Never let shallots brown or they will become bitter. They make a wonderful flavoring agent in salads, sauces, and dressings.

If shallots are unavailable, substitute a mixture of mild sweet onion and garlic in a pinch. Don't, whatever you do, make a practice of this. There's a decided difference when you use the real thing.

CHIVES

Chives are the fragile ingénues of the onion family. Often mistaken for herbs, chives grow in tufts of delicate, quill-like leaves that closely resemble hollow blades of grass. Only the bright green foliage of the chive plant is edible; it has a subtle oniony flavor famous for sparking the natural taste of food. It grows anywhere from three to nine inches in height.

Don't be misled into thinking that dried or frozen chives are a substitute for the real thing. Use something other than fresh and the flavor does not come through. While they may look pleasingly green, they are disappointingly tasteless. The only delicious chive is the fresh chive gathered into a bunch and finely diced for sensational flavoring.

Grocery stores and plant shops sell chives potted, so why not grow your own? It's a gourmet touch that everyone can afford. Find a spot in your kitchen with lots of light and a sunny exposure. Keep the plant well watered. That's all the tender loving care it requires. One small pot yields a wealth of wonderful flavoring and garnishing. It enhances the kitchen decor immeasurably.

I am never without a pot on my kitchen windowsill to ensure a fresh supply all winter. When chives bloom early in spring, their flowers are a joy to behold. Spectacularly beautiful with rounded globes of soft purple blooms, they dazzle the eye. If you can bear to pick them, toss the flowers into a salad. They can be eaten, and they have a delicate oniony flavor and crunchy texture.

To fix chives, wash them in cool water and pat dry on a paper towel. Using sharp scissors, snip them carefully to lessen the bruising of the delicate stems. You can involve chives with just about everything. Sometimes I find myself about to sprinkle them as a garnish on chocolate pudding.

For a real taste treat, mix chives with sour cream and put a dollop on baked potatoes, stir into cottage cheese, blend with butter and spread on freshly baked bread, fold into scrambled eggs or omelets, combine with cheese spreads, toss into salads and dressings, sprinkle into sauces and gravies, and scatter them on just about everything—except chocolate pudding.

GARLIC

Lusty, demonstrative, and assertive—garlic is the extrovert of the allium gang. Never take it for granted or underestimate its ability. Depending on how it's used, garlic can titillate your taste buds or knock your socks off.

Revered or reviled (there are those who keep their distance with a vehemence), garlic has been around for over five thousand years. Indications are that there's even more of a garlicky future in store. Consumption of this zesty member of the onion family has increased one thousand percent during the past ten years.

Garlic bulbs grow entirely underground. After harvesting, they

The Crusaders, returning to Europe from the Holy Land, brought back garlic and introduced its aromatic pungency to the continent, where monks and herbalists proceeded to cultivate the bulbs.

To impart a touch of garlic (skeptics insist there's no such thing) to the salad, rub the inside of the bowl with the cut side of a garlic clove before adding the ingredients. Or rub a dry crust of bread on all sides with a cut garlic clove, then pop it in with the rest of the makings. In the best of salad circles, it's called a chapon. Always keep a head of fresh garlic handy. Never use garlic or onion salts or powders. They become rancid and stale quickly and ruin otherwise excellent salads in a couple of shakes.

are allowed to dry out until the sheathing around the bulbs becomes a parchment-like husk. This outer covering encloses a varied number of purplish cloves that fit together like the sections of a tangerine. One bud contains anywhere from eight to twelve cloves. Colors vary from pink to purple, white, or white with purplish streaks.

Select only plump, dry, firm garlic bulbs with wrinkle-free, unbroken skins for your shopping basket. Smaller bulbs are just as high in flavor and quality. They also may be less costly. Be sure that none of the cloves has pulled away from the bulb. Reject any with green sprouts or yellowed, soft cloves. Remember—the fresher the garlic, the milder the taste. When harvested, garlic is often braided into garlands. Decorated with a festive bow, they make unique gifts. Garlic lovers will be ecstatic.

Always use fresh garlic! It's available year round and nothing—whether it is garlic powder, paste, salt, dehydrated flakes, or bottled juice—bears the slightest resemblance to Nature's original creation. Garlic salt is exactly what it claims to be—salt. The rest of these processed substitutes tend to become acrid and tasteless within a very short time and will ruin a perfectly good recipe.

To peel a whole garlic clove easily, dip it into boiling water to loosen the skin. Or you can peel and partially crush a clove by thumping it with the flat side of a chef's knife. The skin pops off. Use a sharp chef's knife for best results when mincing garlic. A food processor or blender does a spiffy job of transforming peeled cloves into purée.

For best results when the recipe calls for crushed cloves, use a garlic press. The results will enslave you forever. To use one, place an unpeeled clove, cut in half if you prefer, in the press. Just squeeze. If the press is not self-cleaning (some are), rinse immediately, before the leftover particles have a chance to dry out and plug the holes. Remember that crushed garlic has about three times the impact of chopped or minced.

Heat and handling affect garlic's potency. Cooked long and slowly, it takes on a mild, delicate flavor and loses its assertiveness. Less flavor is imparted by whole cloves when popped into dishes and allowed to cook for varying degrees of time. Impale the cloves on toothpicks for easy retrieving. Garlic is at its most robust when used raw in minced or crushed form; the more it's cut, the more flavor it releases.

Garlic burns easily. Make sure that the pan and shortening are not too hot when sautéing. Burned garlic will impart a bitter taste.

Garlic's middle name is Versatility. Use it raw in appetizers, salads, and dressings. Simmer it in stews, soups, sauces, seasonings, and main dishes. Dress up vegetable dishes with a garlic crumb topping, whip it with butter and slather it on French bread for garlic toast. Permeate a roast with garlic flavor by tucking tiny slivers into slashes in the meat, or pop a peeled clove into a bag of potato chips for several hours for a garlicky taste treat. Or add a peeled garlic clove to the oil for popping popcorn—delicious!

Balzac suggested that even the cook should be rubbed with garlic.

Worried about garlic breath? Rinse your mouth out with a mixture of lemon juice and water. Chew on orange peel or a clove of cinnamon. Eat an apple. Or think positively like garlic lovers—it's chic to reek!

> Archeologists in search of King Tut's remains unearthed a profusion of garlic cloves entombed with the mummy to ensure his everlasting youth and sexual prowess in the great beyond.

MAKING ONION GARNISHES

Decorative garnishes lend a finishing touch to foods. To most of us, a sprinkling of fresh parsley, a dusting of paprika, or a topping of grated cheese are second nature, and throughout the book you will find suggestions for garnishing with snipped fresh chives, diced scallions, and chopped sweet onions to add bright accents.

Whole onions and scallions become attractive, edible garnishes in no time at all with the help of a sharp, pointed knife and some

Inspired by the onion's form and symmetry, architects designed the onion dome that adorns many mosques and churches throughout the world. The Cathedral of Assumption in Moscow, with its five onion domes, is an imposing sight on the Russian skyline. Built during the Czarist regime, this magnificent church was used for the coronation of royalty.

ice water. Let your imagination and creativity follow their natural inclinations.

SCALLION RUFFLES Trim off and discard the root ends of a bunch of scallions. Cut off all but 4 inches of the green tops. Using a sharp, pointed knife, cut the green stems into thin slivers down to the white bulbs. Soak in ice water until the stems begin to curl. Drain and decorate.

ONION MUM Peel a medium-size onion, but leave the root end intact. Place the onion root-end down on a cutting board. Make a shallow X in the top of each onion. Using this as a guide, cut the onion into quarters to within ¼ inch of the root end. Slice each quarter downward into thin wedges to form petals. Soak in ice water until the petals begin to open. Drain and decorate. For colored flowers, add red, yellow, or orange food coloring to the water.

ONION CHAIN Peel and slice small onions into ⅛-inch slices. Separate into rings. Cut through one side of half of the rings. Link the rings, alternating cut and uncut rings. Crisp in ice water. Use to decorate meat and salad platters.

ONION CUPS Hollow out peeled onions to make cups to hold dips or relishes. Trim the root end to make a flat base for the onion to stand on.

ONION-RING HOLDERS Peel and slice an extra large Spanish onion to make rings of graduating sizes to hold vinaigretted asparagus stalks upright.

APPETIZERS

APPETIZERS SET THE STAGE for the show to follow. Whether it's an intimate buffet for special friends, a casual gathering of the clan, or a formal dinner for business associates, these bite-size tidbits should pique the appetite while conjuring up a mood of congeniality and relaxation.

A dependable rule of thumb is to stimulate, not satiate, the appetite when offering guests a selection of delectable morsels as a prelude to the meal ahead. Unless, of course, the event is a festive cocktail party. For an all-appetizer affair, you can throw caution to the winds and dazzle invitees with a regal array of hors d'oeuvres, canapés, snacks, nibbles, and dips. It's the only way to go to appease hunger pangs and counteract the effect of cocktails on an empty stomach.

Whatever the occasion, look to members of the onion family to provide unique flavors, textures, and ideas for appetizers that pleasure the palate and enhance your reputation as a host or hostess.

If you are concerned about onion breath, float sprigs of parsley in a crystal bowl of ice water for guests to chew on. The chlorophyll in the parsley helps to diminish the onion aroma and goes a long way to promoting group charisma if, perish forbid, there are non-onion lovers present. Better yet, convert them!

Members of the Roman aristocracy, believing garlic to be an aphrodisiac, consumed it in monumental quantities at a never-ending succession of social gatherings. While providing a lucrative livelihood for plebeian farmers who worked night and day to supply demands, this obsession gave real meaning to the name by which these affairs came to be known—Roman orgies.

ONION & PARSLEY WREATHS

PREPARATION: 30 MINUTES
MARINATING: 4–6 HOURS
YIELD: 24 SANDWICHES

3 small sweet onions, sliced wafer thin
1 lemon, sliced wafer thin
¼ cup olive oil
¼ cup vegetable oil
¼ cup white wine vinegar
2 tablespoons fresh lemon juice
24 slices thin rye bread
½ cup garlic mayonnaise (*Aïoli*, page 145)
1 cup finely chopped fresh parsley

An absolutely marvelous appetizer with back-for-seconds taste appeal. Onion skeptics will succumb immediately. Use your sharpest knife and make the onion slices almost transparent.

In a glass or ceramic bowl, layer the onion and lemon slices. End with a layer of lemon. Whisk together the oils, vinegar, and lemon juice. Pour over the onion mixture. Marinate 4–6 hours, basting frequently with the marinade.

To serve, drain the onion slices. Using a 2-inch cutter, shape each slice of bread into 2 rounds. Spread one side of each round with garlic mayonnaise. Layer several thin onion slices on each of 24 rounds of rye. Make sure the slices do not overlap the bread rounds. Top with the remaining rounds to make sandwiches. Press together firmly. Using thumb and forefinger, roll the edges in garlic mayonnaise and then in chopped parsley to make a green wreath. Arrange the rounds on platters with wax paper. Cover with plastic wrap, and chill for 1 hour.

SCALLION SKINNY DIP

PREPARATION: 10 MINUTES
YIELD: 3 CUPS

2 cups low-fat cottage cheese
1 cup plain low-fat yogurt
2 tablespoons grated sweet onion
¼ cup chopped scallions with greens
2 tablespoons chopped fresh parsley
1 clove garlic, crushed
1 hard-boiled egg, quartered
1 tablespoon fresh lemon juice
freshly ground black pepper

Easy on the waistline, this piquant dip is the answer to a dieter's prayer. Serve it with crunchy, raw vegetables or crisp apple slices and scoop it up with wild abandon and a clear conscience.

Combine the cheese, yogurt, onion, scallions, parsley, garlic, egg, and lemon juice in a food processor or blender. Whirl until blended. Remove the mixture and season to taste with pepper. Serve with a chilled assortment of any of the following: broccoli florets, cauliflorets, carrot strips, celery sticks, sliced mushrooms, snow peas, cucumber slices, sweet onion slices, cherry tomatoes, green beans, zucchini slices, bell pepper strips.

MARINATED SHRIMP & RED ONION RINGS

PREPARATION: 15 MINUTES
MARINATING: 8 HOURS
YIELD: 20–24

1 pound cooked, cleaned medium
  shrimp
2 red Italian onions, thinly sliced
1 lemon, thinly sliced
½ cup sliced black and green olives
¼ cup olive oil
¼ cup vegetable oil
2 tablespoons fresh lemon juice
½ cup red wine vinegar
¼ cup finely minced fresh parsley
1 clove garlic, minced
½ teaspoon dry mustard
1 tablespoon chopped fresh dill or ½
  teaspoon dried dillweed
1 bay leaf, halved
freshly ground black pepper
romaine lettuce leaves
parsley sprigs
lemon wedges

Allow at least eight hours marinating time to mingle the flavors of this shrimply wonderful appetizer. Impale each shrimp on a decorative party pick for an eye-catching presentation and serve with black and green garlic olives.

In a glass or ceramic bowl, layer the shrimp, onion slices, lemon slices, and olives. Whisk together the oils, lemon juice, vinegar, parsley, garlic, mustard, and dill. Add the bay leaf. Season to taste with pepper. Pour the mixture over the shrimp. Toss lightly to coat each shrimp. Cover tightly and refrigerate for 8 hours. Mix gently occasionally. To serve, remove the shrimp from the marinade. Arrange on a lettuce lined platter with the onion slices and sliced olives. Garnish with parsley sprigs and lemon wedges. Serve chilled.

ONION & EGGPLANT APPETIZER WITH PINE NUTS

PREPARATION: 20 MINUTES
COOKING: 30–35 MINUTES
YIELD: 4–5 CUPS

1 eggplant, 1½–2 pounds
2 tablespoons butter
2 tablespoons olive oil
1 cup chopped sweet onion
1 cup thinly sliced celery
1 cup chopped red or green pepper
3 cloves garlic, minced
2 tomatoes, chopped
2 tablespoons chopped fresh parsley
2 teaspoons chopped fresh basil or ½
    teaspoon dried
1 tablespoon chopped fresh oregano
    or 1 teaspoon dried
2 tablespoons fresh lemon juice
1 tablespoon red wine vinegar
freshly ground black pepper to taste
½ cup small stuffed olives
½ cup pine nuts, toasted
lemon wedges
toasted pita bread wedges

Often called Caponatina, this spicy concoction of onion, eggplant, tomatoes, garlic, and olives is a passion in our household. Once you make your own, any store-bought substitute pales by comparison. Allow lots of mingling time for the ingredients and toast the pine nuts for extra flavor.

Trim the end slices from the eggplant. Cut it into ¼-inch-thick slices. In a large, heavy skillet, melt the butter with the oil. Cook the eggplant slices, several at a time, until golden brown on both sides. Remove and drain on paper towels.

Cook and stir the onion, celery, green pepper, and garlic in the same skillet until tender crisp. Add the tomatoes, parsley, basil, and oregano. Cook until slightly thickened. Remove from heat. Chop the eggplant. Combine with the onion and tomato mixture and mix well.

Stir in the lemon juice and vinegar. Season to taste with the pepper. Mix in the whole olives. Refrigerate, covered, until the flavors blend. To serve, sprinkle with toasted pine nuts. Garnish with lemon wedges and toasted pita bread wedges.

NOTE: To toast the pine nuts, place in a small skillet over low heat. Cook, stirring constantly, until lightly browned.

HAM BITES DIABLO

PREPARATION: 15 MINUTES
YIELD: 2–2½ CUPS

1 pound cooked, smoked ham, cubed
1 clove garlic, minced
2 tablespoons chopped fresh parsley
½ cup chopped scallions with greens
4 tablespoons chopped sweet onion
3 tablespoons mayonnaise
1 small package (3 ounces) cream
  cheese, softened
1 teaspoon prepared mustard (or to
  taste)
2 tablespoons sweet pickle relish
1 tablespoon lemon juice
dash curry
apple, cucumber, and Bermuda onion
  slices
chopped fresh chives

If there's a vestige of ham around, I experience an uncontrollable urge to make this wonderful appetizer. It's a long-standing food fetish of mine. In pre-processor days, I cranked it through an antique food grinder with the same delicious and addictive results.

Grind or process the ham, garlic, parsley, scallions, and onion together. In a separate bowl, whisk together the mayonnaise, cream cheese, mustard, relish, lemon juice, and curry. Stir in the ground ham mixture. Refrigerate, covered, to blend. Serve on thin, crisp slices of apple, cucumber, or onion. Garnish with chopped chives.

POTTED CHEESE & ONION SPREAD

PREPARATION: 15 MINUTES
YIELD: 2 CUPS

½ cup beer
1 pound white Cheddar cheese, grated
1 tablespoon grated sweet onion
2 tablespoons snipped fresh chives
½ teaspoon dry mustard
2 tablespoons finely chopped fresh
   parsley
1 teaspoon lemon juice
4 tablespoons butter, softened
3 cloves garlic, peeled and halved

An all-time favorite in English pubs. This spicy spread with its glorious combination of flavors is even better for the aging. Refrigerate for at least a week, if patience permits, before serving.

In a blender or food processor, combine the beer, cheese, onion, chives, mustard, parsley, lemon juice, and butter. Process until blended and smooth. Spoon one-third of the mixture into a crock or jar with an airtight cover. Push 2 garlic halves into the mixture. Add another one-third of the mixture. Insert 2 more garlic halves. Fill the crock with the remaining cheese mixture and the remaining garlic cloves. Cover with a circle of wax paper cut to the size of the jar top. Cover and seal tightly. Age in the refrigerator before using. Serve with crisp crackers.

VARIATION

BRANDIED CHEESE AND ONION SPREAD. Substitute ½ cup of brandy or cognac for the beer. Prepare as directed.

CHEESE & CHIVE PARTY PUFFS

PREPARATION: 30 MINUTES
BAKING: 30–35 MINUTES
YIELD: 36 PUFFS

1 cup milk
½ cup butter
¼ cup finely minced fresh chives
½ cup finely diced lean, cooked ham
1 cup unbleached, all-purpose flour
¾ cup grated Cheddar cheese
4 eggs, room temperature

Our version of gougère—*a traditional pastry delight from France. Piping hot from the oven, they cannot be denied. Ensure success by fearlessly adding the flour all at once and beating ever so briskly.*

Preheat oven to 400°F. In a large saucepan, combine the milk, butter, chives, and ham. Bring to a boil slowly. Remove from the heat. Combine the flour and cheese. Add to the milk mixture all at once. Stir vigorously with a wooden spoon until the mixture leaves the side of the pan and forms a ball. Cool slightly. Add the eggs, one at a time. Beat well after each addition until batter is smooth and glossy. Drop by rounded teaspoonfuls onto an ungreased baking sheet, 2 inches apart. Gently shape into balls. Bake for 10 minutes. Reduce the heat to 350°F and bake until puffy and golden, 20–25 minutes. Turn off the oven. Remove the puffs and pierce with a fork to release the steam. Return to the oven to dry for 10 minutes. Serve warm.

CHEDDAR CHEESE & SHALLOT TARTLETS

PREPARATION: 30 MINUTES
BAKING: 20–25 MINUTES
YIELD: 30–36 TARTLETS

½ cup butter
½ pound small, white mushrooms, cleaned, trimmed, and finely chopped
2 shallots, finely diced
1 cup cream
¼ cup port wine
¾ cup grated Cheddar cheese
1 tablespoon unbleached, all-purpose flour
2 egg yolks, beaten
1 tablespoon chopped fresh parsley
Cream Cheese Pastry

Famous for their vanishing act, these scrumptious mini-tarts disappear in one bite. The creamy filling, delicately seasoned with shallots and laced with port wine, nestles in light-as-a-feather cream cheese pastry. Magnifique!

Preheat oven to 375°F. In a large, heavy skillet, melt two tablespoons of the butter. Sauté the mushrooms for 5 minutes. Add the shallots and cook until tender. Do not brown. Whisk together the cream and port wine. Stir into the mushrooms. Cook until the mixture thickens slightly. Gradually add the cheese and mix well. Remove from the heat. Melt the remaining butter and whisk together with the egg yolks, flour, and parsley. Combine with the mushroom mixture.

Roll out the pastry dough to 1/16-inch thickness. Cut out 2-inch circles. Combine and reroll the scraps to make additional circles. Press into the bottoms and up the sides of mini-muffin pans. Fill each shell with a heaping tablespoon of the mixture. Bake for 20–25 minutes or until the filling puffs and the tops are golden brown. Cool slightly and serve while still warm.

CREAM CHEESE PASTRY

2 packages (3 ounces) cream cheese, softened
½ cup butter, softened
2 cups unbleached, all-purpose flour
¼ teaspoon salt
Ice water to moisten

Blend together the cream cheese and the butter in large bowl. Add the flour and the salt. Using a fork, blend the cheese and butter mixture into the flour until it resembles small peas. Sprinkle small amounts of ice water to moisten until the mixture forms a ball. With hands, shape into 2 flat balls. Wrap in wax paper and refrigerate.

LOBSTER-FILLED PARTY PUFFS

PREPARATION: 20 MINUTES
CHILLING: 1 HOUR
YIELD: 36 PUFFS

1½ cups cooked lobster meat, finely
   diced
1 tablespoon fresh lemon juice
¼ cup mayonnaise
½ cup sour cream
2 tablespoons finely minced sweet
   onion
½ cup finely minced celery
1 tablespoon minced fresh parsley
¼ teaspoon dry mustard
1 Recipe *Cheese and Chive Party
   Puffs*, page 35 (omit the ham and
   cheese)

Split these feathery-light shells and tuck them full of lobster filling laced with sour cream and chopped sweet onion. To prevent "The Soggies," fill the puffs at the very last minute. Not to worry from then on—they won't be around long enough.

Sprinkle the lobster meat with the lemon juice. Toss to coat. Whisk together the mayonnaise, sour cream, onion, celery, parsley, and mustard. Fold into the lobster meat. Refrigerate, covered, for 1 hour. Just before serving, split the puffs and remove any soft centers. Fill with the lobster mixture and serve immediately.

STUFFED MUSHROOMS SICILIAN

PREPARATION: 30 MINUTES
BAKING: 15–20 MINUTES
YIELD: 24 MUSHROOMS

24 medium-size mushrooms, cleaned
   and trimmed
½ pound mild bulk Italian sausage
½ cup finely diced scallions with
   greens
1 clove garlic, crushed
1½ teaspoons chopped fresh oregano
   or ½ teaspoon dried
1 teaspoon Worcestershire sauce
¾ cup shredded Swiss cheese
½ cup finely chopped hazelnuts
2 tablespoons olive oil
Hungarian paprika

A savory mixture of melted Swiss cheese, zesty Italian sausage, and chopped hazelnuts piled high on tender mushroom caps. For successful stuffing, select firm white mushrooms, uniform in size, with caps tucked down close to the stem.

Preheat oven to 400°F. With a small, sharp knife remove the mushroom stems. Leave a smooth, rounded cavity to stuff. Set the caps aside. Chop the stems finely and reserve. In a large, heavy skillet, crumble the sausage. Cook, using a wooden spoon to break up large pieces, until browned. Drain and discard excess fat. Stir in the chopped mushroom stems, scallions, garlic, oregano, and Worcestershire sauce. Cook until all moisture evaporates. Remove from the heat. Stir in half the cheese and all the hazelnuts. Brush each mushroom cap with oil. Fill each cavity with one rounded tablespoon of the sausage mixture. Arrange the caps, single layer, in a shallow baking dish. Sprinkle with the remaining cheese. Dust with paprika. Bake uncovered for 15–20 minutes, or until heated through. Serve hot.

BAKED GARLIC SPREAD

PREPARATION: 10 MINUTES
BAKING: 1 HOUR
YIELD: ½–¾ CUP

2 whole large heads (not cloves) fresh
   garlic
2 tablespoons butter
salt to taste
freshly ground black pepper to taste
sesame crackers

So valuable was the aromatic garlic bulb that well into the eighteenth century Siberian villagers in Russia paid taxes of garlic to their landowners.

To experience is to believe. Garlic cloves, baked long and slowly, develop a mild, sweet flavor delicate enough to convert skeptics and make garlic lovers ecstatic. Gently pop the cloves out of their skins for an instant spread—delightfully creamy and unforgettably good.

Preheat oven to 325°F. Wrap each head of garlic in foil to completely enclose it, but leave enough room for the cloves to expand. Seal the edges. Bake for 1 hour at 325°F. Cool and remove from the foil. Gently squeeze each clove out of its skin and discard the skins. Mash with butter and season to taste. Spread on crisp sesame crackers.

VARIATION

For a low-cal spread, eliminate the butter and mash each clove directly onto the cracker after removing the skin.

CHOPPED CHICKEN LIVER SAVOURY WITH SWEET ONION

PREPARATION: 20 MINUTES
COOKING: 10 MINUTES
CHILLING: 2 HOURS
YIELD: 2 CUPS

2 cups finely chopped sweet onion
1 clove garlic, minced
1 pound chicken livers, washed and
   trimmed
1 cup chicken stock
2 tablespoons chopped fresh parsley
1 bay leaf
1 teaspoon grated lemon peel
2 tablespoons butter, softened
2 hard-boiled eggs, chopped
2 anchovy fillets
dash nutmeg
freshly ground black pepper to taste
1 cup whipped cream
curry (optional)
cognac (optional)

A savoury is uniquely British. It is a tasty tidbit served after dessert, believe it or not, to top off the meal. The custom is fast diminishing, so we've converted this all-time favorite into an appetizer. For added zest, include a dash of curry and a goodly splash of cognac during blending.

In a saucepan, combine 1 cup of the onion, the garlic, chicken livers, chicken stock, 1 tablespoon chopped parsley, the bay leaf, and lemon peel. Simmer gently for 10 minutes. Strain the mixture. Reserve the stock. Remove and discard the bay leaf. In a blender or food processor, combine the chicken liver mixture, remaining parsley, butter, eggs, anchovy fillets, nutmeg, and pepper until blended. Add a little chicken stock if needed. Season to taste with curry and cognac. Refrigerate and chill for 20 minutes. Fold in the whipped cream. Refrigerate and chill thoroughly. Serve with crisp crackers and a bowl of the remaining chopped onion for topping.

PICKLED ONION APPETIZERS

PREPARATION: 25 MINUTES
COOKING: 5 MINUTES
MARINATING: 1 WEEK
YIELD: 1½–2 PINTS

2 pounds small, round, ½-inch silverskin pickling onions
2 cups white vinegar
¼ cup brown sugar, firmly packed
1 teaspoon mustard seeds
1 tablespoon fresh dill
1 teaspoon peppercorns
½-inch slice fresh ginger root
1 bay leaf
2 cloves garlic, peeled
fresh dill sprigs

Mellowed in a piquant, spicy marinade for several weeks (the longer, the better), tiny whole pickled onions make great appetizers. Crisp and crunchy, they're ready for popping into soups, stews, salads, dry martinis, or your mouth in rapid succession.

Cover the unpeeled onions with boiling water for 3 minutes. Drain, cool, and peel. Combine the vinegar, sugar, mustard seeds, dill, peppercorns, ginger root, bay leaf, and garlic cloves in a large, non-corrosive saucepan. Bring to a boil. Add the onions and simmer for 3 minutes. Transfer the onions with a slotted spoon into clean, glass half-pint jars. Fill ⅔ full. Cover with the cooled vinegar mixture to ¼ inch from the top. Add a dill sprig to each jar. Cap the jars and seal tightly. Refrigerate for several weeks (at least 1) before serving.

SALADS & DRESSINGS

Put some sunshine into your meals all year round—serve salads! It's such a glorious way to transform nature's bounty into healthy eating. Salads not only perk up appetites and brighten the table, they contribute a storehouse of life-sustaining vitamins, minerals, and roughage to the diet.

Cooks everywhere are combining meat, fish, poultry, cheese, eggs, pasta, and fruits with garden vegetables in myriad ways to create salads for every occasion. Include some imagination with the ingredients and there's no end to the variety of combinations you can conjure up. Salad making provides the perfect opportunity for inventive resourcefulness and derring-do.

When it comes to spectacular salad making, freshness spells the difference. Growing your own vegetables is the ultimate insurance, but being selective in the produce section comes in a close second. Choose crisp, bright greens and fresh, crunchy vegetables. Refrigerate them in the crisper or in a plastic bag with a paper towel tucked inside to absorb excess moisture. Scallions, leeks, and chives are perishable; they require refrigeration. Dry onions, shallots and garlic do not; storing them in the refrigerator encourages mildew and rotting.

When to serve salads? Whenever you please. Their appearance at the table is strictly a matter of preference. Let salads be a light, refreshing meal-starter to whet the appetite. Or serve one

Always serve greens clean, cold, crisp, and dry. Use a salad spinner to whirl away excess moisture. It guarantees that the dressing will cling with tenacity. Solve the "chop or tear" dilemma easily. Tear the greens when preparing them in advance. The edges won't darken as quickly. If you plan to serve right away, go ahead and chop. It's quick and easy, and will not affect the flavor at all. Be sure to use a bowl large enough for tossing. To keep greens from bruising, use a gentle touch when mixing the ingredients. I try to imagine that I'm conducting Brahms' Lullaby with the Boston Pops.

as a colorful counterpoint to accompany the entrée. Use a salad as a respite to cleanse the palate before dessert arrives. If it's robust enough, give the salad star billing and let it stand alone as the main event. Don't discount the idea of serving one for dessert. It's really not so much when a salad makes the scene but how.

It is in the salad bowl where the miracles wrought by onions, leeks, scallions, shallots, chives, and garlic make the difference between mediocrity and magnificence. So slice, dice, mince, grate, snip, julienne, chop, and plop alliums into your salads with unbounded enthusiasm!

CONFETTI COLESLAW

PREPARATION: 20 MINUTES
CHILLING: 60 MINUTES
YIELD: 6–8 SERVINGS

3 cups shredded green cabbage
1 cup shredded red cabbage
½ cup peeled, grated parsnip
½ cup grated carrot
½ cup chopped sweet red onion
½ cup chopped green pepper
½ cup diced apple, peeled and cored
½ cup plain yogurt
¾ cup mayonnaise
1 talbespoon honey
3 tablespoons fresh lemon juice
¼ cup heavy cream
½ teaspoon mustard seeds
¼ cup chopped peanuts

The nutty sweetness of parsnip and tart piquancy of yogurt lend a distinctive touch to this rainbow-colored slaw. Dollop each serving with sour cream and thank heaven for cabbages and sweet red onion.

In a large bowl, combine the cabbages, parsnip, carrot, onion, green pepper, and apple. Whisk together the yogurt, mayonnaise, honey, lemon juice, cream, and mustard seeds. Fold into the slaw mixture. Toss well to mix. Refrigerate for at least 1 hour. Sprinkle with the chopped peanuts and serve immediately.

WELSH LEEK & TOMATO SALAD VINAIGRETTE

PREPARATION: 20 MINUTES
STANDING: 30 MINUTES
YIELD: 4 SERVINGS

The Welsh love leeks with a passion, so much so that leeks became the national emblem of Wales. Serve this earthy delicacy and you will understand why.

8 medium leeks with tender greens,
　sliced into ½-inch rings
lettuce leaves
3 large, ripe tomatoes, cut into small
　wedges
Vinaigrette Dressing
red wine vinegar
2 hard-boiled eggs, chopped

Steam the leeks in a covered saucepan until tender crisp. Lift the lid several times to retain the color. Do not overcook or the leeks become mushy. Rinse immediately in cold water. Drain well. Arrange on a lettuce-lined platter. Surround with tomato wedges. Sprinkle most of the dressing over the leeks. Cover loosely and let stand at room temperature for 30 minutes. Baste occasionally with the remaining dressing. Before serving, drizzle vinegar evenly over the leeks and tomatoes, to taste. Sprinkle with chopped egg. Serve at once.

VINAIGRETTE DRESSING

2 tablespoons olive oil
2 tablespoons light vegetable oil
2 tablespoons fresh lemon juice
1 tablespoon chopped fresh parsley
2 teaspoons honey
½ small clove garlic, crushed
1 teaspoon Worcestershire sauce
¼ teaspoon dried tarragon
¼ teaspoon freshly ground black
　pepper

Whisk together the ingredients and mix well. Let the flavors mingle before using.

PICKLED BEET, ONION, & HERRING SALAD

PREPARATION: 30–35 MINUTES
MARINATING: 30 MINUTES
CHILLING: 2 HOURS
YIELD: 4–6 SERVINGS

2 cups diced cooked beets
2 cups diced cooked potatoes
1 cup chopped sweet red Italian onion
2 tablespoons chopped fresh parsley
¼ cup olive oil
¼ cup light vegetable oil
3 tablespoons red wine vinegar
1 tablespon fresh lemon juice
¼ cup chopped dill pickle
1 tart green apple, peeled, cored, and
   diced
1 cup pickled herring fillets (8-ounce
   jar)
lettuce leaves
1 tablespoon capers
2 hard-boiled eggs, sliced lengthwise
Creamy Horseradish Dressing (page
   53)

A continental delicacy with international appeal. European restaurants often feature this superb salad as a specialty on their menus. Try cooking the beets and potatoes from scratch. You'll find a world of difference in the taste and texture.

In a large bowl, combine the beets, potatoes, onion, and 1 tablespoon parsley. Whisk together the oils, vinegar, and lemon juice. Pour over the beet mixture. Mix gently and marinate for 30 minutes. Drain off the marinade and reserve. Add the pickle and apple to the mixture. Chop the herring into bite-size pieces. Gently fold into the beet mixture. Cover and refrigerate for 2 hours. To serve, allow the mixture to come to room temperature. Spoon onto lettuce-lined plates. Garnish with egg slices, capers, and remaining parsley. Serve with a bowlful of Creamy Horseradish Dressing. For a colorful accent, swirl a tablespoon of the beet marinade into the dressing just before serving.

PORTUGUESE POTATO & SARDINE SALAD

PREPARATION: 45 MINUTES
CHILLING: 30–60 MINUTES
YIELD: 4–6 SERVINGS

6 new potatoes
1 cup diced celery, including leaves
¼ cup chopped scallions with greens
½ cup chopped sweet onion
2 cans Portuguese boneless, skinless
    sardines
2 tablespoons lemon juice
½ teaspoon dry mustard
¼ cup mayonnaise
¼ cup sour cream
1 tablespoon white wine vinegar
¼ teaspoon freshly ground black
    pepper
salt to taste
lettuce leaves
1 sweet red Italian onion, thinly sliced
2 tablespoons chopped fresh parsley
10 *Garlic Olives* (see next page)

Portuguese sardines, those plump, savory little creatures from the sea, transform an ordinary potato salad into a taste sensation.

In a large saucepan, cook the potatoes in their skins until tender. Drain, cool, and peel. Slice into cubes in a large bowl. Add the celery, scallions, and chopped onion. Toss lightly. Drain the sardines. In a small bowl, mash 1 can of sardines with 1 tablespoon lemon juice. Reserve. Whisk together the mustard, mayonnaise, sour cream, vinegar, pepper, and salt to taste. Stir in the mashed sardines. Gently fold the sardine mixture into the potatoes. Toss lightly. Line a salad bowl with lettuce leaves. Mound the salad in the center. Sprinkle the remaining sardines with 1 tablespoon of lemon juice and arrange them like spokes of a wheel on the salad. Sprinkle with the chopped parsley. Rim the bowl with the onion rings and garlic olives. Serve at once.

GARLIC OLIVES

2 cups green or black olives with pits
½ bay leaf
1 teaspoon fresh rosemary
1 teaspoon grated lemon rind
4 peeled and halved garlic cloves
½ cup olive oil

Drain the olives and reserve the liquid. Place olives in a 1-pint jar with the bay leaf, rosemary, lemon rind, and garlic cloves. Add the olive oil and enough reserved liquid to cover the olives. Seal the jar with a lid. Shake the jar to distribute the flavorings. Store for several days in a cool place to allow the flavors to mingle.

The oil in which the olives mature develops a delicious flavor. Use it for cooking or in salads.

TIPSY SHRIMP BOATS

PREPARATION: 30 MINUTES
CHILLING: 30 MINUTES
YIELD: 6 SERVINGS

1 pound cooked, cleaned shrimp
3 tablespoons fresh lemon juice
3 ripe avocados
2 tablespoons chopped fresh parsley
3 tablespoons diced scallions with
  greens
⅓ cup mayonnaise
⅓ cup heavy cream
1 teaspoon minced shallot
¼ cup white rum
½ cup coarsely chopped pistachio nuts

No other salad matches this one for sheer elegance of taste and temptation. If girth permitted, I would indulge every day of the week. Use the black, gnarled variety of avocado and sprinkle the luscious rum-laced filling with crunchy pistachio nuts.

Halve the shrimps and sprinkle with 1 tablespoon lemon juice. Slice the avocados in half lengthwise. Remove and discard the pits. Carefully scoop the avocado meat in a bowl. Sprinkle with 1 tablespoon lemon juice. Brush the inside of each avocado shell with the remaining lemon juice. Cover the shells with plastic wrap and refrigerate. Dice the avocado meat into small chunks. Combine with 1 tablespoon of parsley, the scallions, and the shrimp pieces. Whisk together the mayonnaise, cream, shallot, and rum. Fold into the shrimp mixture. Cover and refrigerate for 30 minutes. To serve, spoon the shrimp mixture into the avocado halves. Garnish with the pistachio nuts and remaining parsley. Serve immediately.

POLYNESIAN MARINATED FISH SALAD

PREPARATION: 20 MINUTES
MARINATING: 2 HOURS
YIELD: 4–6 SERVINGS

1½ pounds ocean fish fillets, cut into
    ½-inch pieces
1 onion, sliced into rings
juice of 1 lemon
juice of 1 lime
1 tablespoon finely minced fresh gin-
    ger root
½ teaspoon freshly ground black
    pepper
½ cup *Coconut Milk*
1 small sweet red onion, chopped
½ cup chopped green bell pepper
¼ cup scallions, chopped with greens
2 tomatoes, peeled and chopped
½ cup grated cucumber
lettuce leaves
2 tablespoons chopped fresh parsley

I first tasted this exotic salad years ago in the South Pacific. It's a mainstay of the islanders' diet. They "cook" the fish in lime juice and use fresh coconut milk. Our version improvises a bit, but it's every bit as delicious. Use ocean, not freshwater, fish for best results.

In a large skillet, cover the fish with water. Simmer for 3–4 minutes. Drain and rinse with cold water. Pat dry. Layer half the onion rings over the bottom of a shallow, non-metal dish. Arrange the fish on top. Scatter the remaining rings over the fish. Combine the lime and lemon juice, ginger root, and black pepper. Spoon over the fish. Cover and refrigerate for 2 hours. Baste several times. Drain off the juices and discard. Remove the onion rings and discard. Pour the Coconut Milk over the fish. Combine the chopped red onion, green pepper, scallions, tomatoes, and cucumber. Add to the fish mixture. Mix gently. Season to taste. Arrange the mixture on lettuce-lined plates. Sprinkle with chopped parsley.

COCONUT MILK

Purée 1½ cups fresh grated or dried grated coconut, unsweetened, and 6 tablespoons milk in a blender or food processor. Remove and let stand for 30 minutes. Strain the mixture through cheesecloth. Squeeze out any excess moisture. Reserve the milk and discard the coconut. Makes about ½ cup.

STUFFED PEPPER RINGS ON ROMAINE

PREPARATION: 20 MINUTES
CHILLING: 3 HOURS
YIELD: 4–6 SERVINGS

1 large green bell pepper
1 large red bell pepper
8 ounces ricotta cheese
½ clove garlic, peeled
2 teaspoons lemon juice
1 tablespoon chopped fresh parsley
3 tablespoons minced scallions with
   greens
½ cup chopped pistachio nuts
1 tablespoon chopped pimiento
1 envelope unflavored gelatin
   (1 tablespoon)
½ cup cold water
romaine lettuce leaves
sliced stuffed olives
Hungarian paprika

Let first the onion flourish there,
Rose among roots, the maiden-fair,
Wine-scented and poetic soul
Of the capacious salad bowl.
   —Robert Louis Stevenson

A salad spectacular that's deliciously different. Melt-in-your-mouth creamy ricotta, flecked with scallions and pistachios, is encircled with crisp rings of red and green peppers. Nestle alternately these colorful slices on a crunchy mattress of lettuce leaves.

Remove the pepper tops and core. Rinse out to remove seeds. Combine the ricotta cheese, garlic, lemon juice, and parsley in a blender or food processor. Blend until smooth. Remove to a bowl and combine with scallions, nuts, and pimiento. Mix the gelatin and cold water. Dissolve over hot water. Add to the cheese mixture and blend well. Spoon the mixture into both peppers. Cover with plastic wrap and refrigerate for 3 hours. To serve, cut each pepper crosswise into ½-inch slices. Arrange alternately colored slices on lettuce leaves. Garnish with stuffed olive slices and dust with paprika. Serve immediately.

SPRING DANDELION & WATERCRESS SALAD

PREPARATION: 35 MINUTES
YIELD: 4 SERVINGS

3 tablespoons white wine vinegar
2 teaspoons honey
1 clove garlic, minced
¼ teaspoon freshly ground black
   pepper
¼ teaspoon dry mustard
4 slices lean bacon
¼ cup chopped sweet onion
4 cups dandelion greens, trimmed,
   washed, and dried
1 bunch watercress, trimmed, washed,
   and dried
½ cup seedless raisins
2 large, ripe tomatoes, sliced
½ cup finely chopped scallions with
   greens

*An early spring safari in search of tender young dande-
lion greens yields a wealth of good eating. Remember that once
the dandelion flowers, the bloom of youth is gone and the leaves
become tough and bitter. Serve them soon after picking with
a sweet and sour bacon dressing to herald the season's return.*

In a small bowl, combine the vinegar, honey, garlic, pepper, and dry mustard. Set aside for 30 minutes. In a large, heavy skillet, sauté the bacon until crisp. Remove, drain, and crumble. Discard all but 2 tablespoons of the drippings. Sauté the onion until tender. Pour in the vinegar mixture, mix well, and remove from the heat. Combine the greens and watercress in a large salad bowl. Combine the vinegar mixture with the raisins. Sprinkle over the greens. Arrange the tomato slices on four individual salad plates. Mound a serving of salad mixture on each slice. Sprinkle with chopped scallions and crumbled bacon. Serve immediately.

CHERRY CHICKEN SALAD

PREPARATION: 20 MINUTES
CHILLING: 2 HOURS
YIELD: 4–6 SERVINGS

2 cups cooked chicken, cubed
¾ cup finely diced celery
2 tablespoons finely diced shallots
1 tablespon finely chopped fresh
  parsley
1 cup dark sweet cherries, pitted and
  halved
½ cup mayonnaise
1 tablespoon wine vinegar
1 tablespoon honey
1 tablespoon fresh lemon juice
2 tablespoons chopped fresh chives
dash ginger
dash curry (optional)
½ cup toasted almonds, chopped
lettuce leaves

Prepare this summery delight early in the day when energy is up and the temperature is down. What a joy to behold and so undeniably scrumptious to eat. It's an extra-special favorite of ours.

In a large bowl, toss the chicken, celery, shallots, parsley, and cherries. Whisk together the mayonnaise, vinegar, honey, lemon juice, chives, ginger, and curry. Fold into the chicken mixture. Chill at least 2 hours. Mix in almonds. Line a serving plate with lettuce leaves. Mound the chicken salad in the center and serve immediately.

MINTED GREEN PEA & SALMON SALAD

PREPARATION: 15 MINUTES
CHILLING: 60 MINUTES
YIELD: 4–6 SERVINGS

So cool and refreshing, this superb salad is as pleasing to the palate as it is to the eye. Whenever possible, I make it with fresh salmon, poached just until it begins to flake—no longer.

1½ cups fresh or frozen peas
¼ cup olive oil
¼ cup light vegetable oil
2 tablespoons red wine vinegar
¼ teaspoon freshly ground black
   pepper
1 clove garlic, minced
1 cup grated carrot
½ cup chopped scallions with greens
½ cup finely diced celery
¼ cup chopped fresh parsley
¼ cup chopped fresh mint leaves
2 tablespoons fresh lemon juice
2 cups cooked red salmon, skinned,
   boned, and flaked
lettuce
2 hard-boiled eggs, chopped
lemon wedges
ripe tomato wedges
mint sprigs

Blanch fresh peas in boiling water for 3–4 minutes. If peas are frozen, thaw quickly in colander under running hot water. Set aside to drain well. In a large bowl, whisk together the oils, vinegar, pepper, and garlic. Stir in the peas, carrot, scallions, celery, parsley, and mint leaves. Sprinkle the lemon juice over the salmon. Gently fold into the vegetable mixture. Cover and refrigerate for at least 1 hour. To serve, mound on a large, lettuce-lined platter. Sprinkle with chopped eggs. Alternate lemon and tomato wedges around the outside. Garnish with mint sprigs. Serve immediately.

BERMUDA ONION DRESSING

PREPARATION: 5 MINUTES
YIELD: 1 CUP

Always brings out the best in any salad.

1 small Bermuda onion, diced
½ clove garlic, minced
1 teaspoon dry mustard
1 teaspoon grated lemon rind
¼ teaspoon freshly ground black
  pepper
¼ cup fresh lemon juice
1 tablespoon chopped fresh dill
1 teaspoon honey
¾ cup light vegetable oil

Place the onion, garlic, mustard, lemon rind, pepper, lemon, juice, dill, and honey in a blender or food processor. Blend until puréed. Trickle in the oil slowly while blending, until the dressing is creamy and all the oil is used. Chill and serve.

CREAMY HORSERADISH DRESSING

PREPARATION: 5 MINUTES
YIELD: 1⅓ CUPS

A zippy, piquant taste that's great on everything.

½ cup sour cream
½ cup ricotta cheese
¼ cup plain yogurt
2 tablespoons prepared horseradish,
  drained
1 tablespoon fresh lemon juice
½ teaspoon Dijon style mustard
1 tablespoon chopped fresh chives
2 tablespoons chopped fresh parsley

Whisk together the ingredients until well blended. Refrigerate until ready to use.

Soups & Stews

THERE IS SOMETHING ABOUT A SIMMERING KETTLE of homemade soup that steams consolation and breathes assurance. Set a pot of chowder to bubbling on the back burner and watch nostrils quiver in anticipation when homecomers open the front door. Nothing whets the appetite and dispels the frustrating effects of a hard day like a whiff of aromatic goodness wafting from the kitchen.

I am a soup-for-all-seasons person, whether it's the robust kind to be attacked with a knife and fork or the velvet variety to be sipped ever so gently with a silver spoon. Soup, to me, embodies keystone cooking with its heritage of wondrous delights. How well I recall the advice of my Scottish granny, lovingly imparted over half a century ago, that good marriages are made in heaven but saved in the soup pot.

Having graduated eons ago from the "waste not, want not" school of cooking, I heartily recommend making soups from scratch. This includes the versatile soup stocks without which it is impossible to simmer soups and stews to superiority. Nothing assures the success of homemade soups or stews like a rich, full-flavored stock. So easy to prepare and store, they are chock full of deep-down goodness and depending on how you season, low in salt.

Do not be intimidated by the common notion that homemade soups and stocks are laborious and difficult to make. Nonsense! The cooking times may be longer, but most soups really don't involve a lot of work. My philosophy has been that the result far outweighs the effort involved: Not only are the taste dividends tremendous, but the costs are gentle to battered budgets.

To prevent sour cream from curdling when adding it to soups or stews, stabilize it first by adding 1 teaspoon of cornstarch or all-purpose flour to each cup of sour cream. Whisk the mixture into the hot cooking liquid and cook over low heat until it is bubbling and thickened.

Prepare and keep a supply of homemade stocks on hand to use as a base in soups, stews, gravies, and sauces or as a rich cooking liquid for braising and poaching.

So relegate your can opener to inactivity in the drawer. Once you compare homemade soups and stocks against their store-bought counterparts, you will have reservations about returning to the salty, additive-laden varieties that line the grocery shelves. There is a world of difference!

Make your own soups with the indispensable help of the onion family. It is in the soup kettle that onions, leeks, shallots, scallions, garlic, and chives splash about with the greatest aplomb. Try to name a soup or stew made without one or more members of the allium family. Virtually impossible!

CHICKEN STOCK

PREPARATION: 10 MINUTES
COOKING: 3½ HOURS
YIELD: 3½ QUARTS

3 pounds chicken parts
4 quarts cold water
4 celery stalks with leaves, chopped
2 large carrots, chopped
1 cup chopped onions
2 leeks, chopped with tender greens
6 peppercorns, cracked
1 bay leaf
1 sprig thyme
2 whole cloves
4 sprigs fresh parsley

Backs, necks, wings—everything but the parson's nose—goes into the soup pot for chicken stock. An indispensable staple in every cook's kitchen.

In a large soup kettle, combine the chicken and cold water. Simmer, uncovered, for 30 minutes. Skim off foam regularly. Add the remaining ingredients. Simmer, partially covered, for 3 hours. Cool and strain. Discard the bones and vegetables. Refrigerate in covered containers. Degrease before using. Store for up to 5 days. Or degrease and freeze in ice cube trays. Transfer to plastic bags, label, and store in freezer.

BROWN BEEF STOCK

PREPARATION: 15 MINUTES
COOKING: 6 HOURS
YIELD: 3½ QUARTS

4 pounds meaty beef bones (include
    shin and marrow bones), cut in
    small pieces
1 meaty shank bone
4 quarts cold water
2 cups chopped onion
1 small leek, washed, trimmed, and
    split in half
1 large carrot, sliced
1 cup chopped tomatoes
1 small onion, unpeeled and stuck
    with 2 whole cloves
8 peppercorns, cracked
1 bay leaf
2 cloves garlic, peeled and halved
1 sprig thyme
4 sprigs parsley

Beef stock, also known as bouillon, is indispensable in cooking. It becomes consommé when reduced by cooking to give a more concentrated flavor.

Roast the bones in a large baking pan at 375°F until well browned. Remove and place in a large soup kettle with 4 quarts of cold water. Deglaze the baking pan with water, scraping up the brown residue. Add to the soup kettle. Simmer, uncovered, for 30 minutes. Skim regularly to remove foam and fat. Add the remaining ingredients. Simmer, partially covered, for 4–5 hours. Cool and strain. Reserve any meat for another use. Discard the bones and vegetables. Refrigerate the stock in covered containers for up to 1 week. Degrease before using. Or remove any fat and freeze in ice cube trays. Store in plastic bags and label.

NOTE: Peppercorns can be cracked by rolling them with a rolling pin a few times. More flavor will be released this way.

GARLIC BROTH

PREPARATION: 15 MINUTES
COOKING: 2 HOURS
YIELD: 1 QUART

1 head of garlic (not clove)
1 quart beef stock
1 teaspoon olive oil
1 small bay leaf
2 tablespoons chopped fresh parsley
¼ teaspoon freshly ground black
    pepper
pinch thyme
pinch sage

History documents that King Henry V of France was anointed with garlic during his birth, to ward off the evil eye.

Don't let the idea of this much garlic strike terror in your heart. As it simmers slowly, garlic becomes sweet, gentle, and delicate in flavor. Taste the fragrant goodness of this broth and you'll make it forevermore.

Separate the garlic head into cloves and peel. Combine with the remaining ingredients in a large soup kettle. Simmer slowly for 2 hours. Remove and discard the garlic cloves and bay leaf. Serve with cooked rice, julienne carrots, tiny sweet peas or mini dumplings. Or cool, freeze in ice cube trays, store in plastic bags, and use as a stock for soups. Label well.

YUGOSLAVIAN GOULASH
(SATARAS)

PREPARATION: 45 MINUTES
COOKING: 2½ HOURS
YIELD: 6–8 SERVINGS

4 tablespoons butter
2 tablespoons vegetable oil
5 cups sliced onions
2 cloves garlic, minced
1 green pepper, cored and thinly sliced
1 cup unbleached, all-purpose flour
2 tablespoons Hungarian paprika
½ teaspoon thyme
½ pound lean veal, cut in 1-inch cubes
½ pound lean pork, cut in 1-inch cubes
1 pound lean beef, cut in 1-inch cubes
3 cups beef stock
¼ teaspoon freshly ground black pepper
½ teaspoon caraway seeds
1 bay leaf
3 ripe tomatoes, peeled and finely chopped
¼ cup chopped fresh parsley
1 cup sour cream
cooked egg noodles

Blessed with a wonderful husband of Yugoslavian heritage, I treasure this old family recipe and make it with unprincipled frequency. Don't worry about the 5 cups of onion—just cook them slowly to sweet, mild perfection.

In a large, heavy skillet, melt 1 tablespoon butter with 1 tablespoon oil. Cook the onions very slowly for 20 minutes, until tender and golden. Add the garlic and pepper slices. Cook 10 minutes longer over low heat. Meanwhile, combine the flour, 1 tablespoon paprika and the thyme in a plastic bag. Add the meat, several cubes at a time, and toss to coat. Reserve any remaining flour mixture. In a large soup kettle, melt the remaining butter with the oil. Brown the meat cubes, a batch at a time. Deglaze the onion mixture in the skillet with 1 cup of beef stock. Transfer to the soup kettle. Stir in the pepper, caraway seeds, bay leaf, tomatoes, and parsley. Add the remaining 2 cups beef stock and mix well. Simmer, covered, over low heat for 2½ hours, stirring occasionally. Mix the reserved flour with some liquid from the pan. Stir into the meat mixture and cook until thickened. Stir in the sour cream just before serving. Season to taste. Serve over hot noodles.

JAMAICAN PEPPER PORK STEW

PREPARATION: 30 MINUTES
COOKING: 1½ HOURS
YIELD: 6–8 SERVINGS

2 tablespoons butter
2 tablespoons olive oil
2 pounds lean pork, cut into 1-inch
    cubes
3 cups coarsely chopped onions
2 cloves garlic, crushed
3 tablespoons uncooked rice
4 ripe tomatoes, peeled and chopped
pinch saffron
½ teaspoon freshly ground black
    pepper
¼ teaspoon cinnamon
3 cups beef stock
2 potatoes, peeled and sliced
¼ cup chopped peanuts
1 green banana or plantain, sliced thin
1 tablespoon molasses
½ cup cream
2 tablespoons chopped fresh cilantro

Caribbean trade winds waft more than the fragrance of tropical flowers. Visitors often pause to inhale the tantalizing aroma of this truly native dish simmering in pots all over the island. Serve it with Calypso music and a flower in your hair.

In a large soup kettle, melt the butter with the olive oil. Brown the pork, a few pieces at a time, on all sides. Remove with slotted spoon and reserve. Sauté the onion, garlic, and rice for 5 minutes. Return the pork to the kettle with the tomatoes, saffron, pepper, cinnamon, and beef stock. Mix well. Simmer slowly, covered, for 1 hour. Add the potatoes and simmer until tender. Stir in the peanuts, banana slices, molasses, cream, and 1 tablespoon cilantro. Heat through but do not boil. Serve at once, sprinkled with the remaining cilantro.

Stews taste even better the second time around. Remove any solidified fat from the top and reheat slowly, stirring often. Increase the heat once the stew liquefies.

A few drops of fresh lemon juice or red-wine vinegar added during the last 10 minutes of cooking perks up the flavor even more.

OXTAIL & ONION STEW

PREPARATION: 45 MINUTES
COOKING: 3½ HOURS
CHILLING: OVERNIGHT
YIELD: 6–8 SERVINGS

3 pounds meaty oxtails, cut in 1½-inch
   joints
½ cup unbleached, all-purpose flour
salt and pepper to taste
2 teaspoons dry mustard
2 tablespoons butter
2 tablespoons vegetable oil
3 cups coarsely chopped onion
1 cup sliced leeks with tender greens
2 cloves garlic, peeled and halved
1 veal knuckle, cracked
3 cups beef stock
3 cups stewed tomatoes with juice
1 cup tomato purée
1 bay leaf
1 teaspoon Worcestershire sauce
1 teaspoon thyme
1 large carrot, peeled and grated
1 cup finely chopped turnip
1 tablespoon pearl barley
2 tablespoons lemon juice
12 small ½-inch silverskin onions,
   peeled
1½ cups finely sliced carrots
1 cup red wine

Typical of rural English cooking, this hale and hearty dish combines deep-down goodness with old-time flavor. It's said to account for John Bull's rotund tummy. Oxtails tend to be on the fatty side, so I begin preparations a day ahead. It makes the stew easier to degrease and less fattening.

Combine the flour, mustard, and seasoning to taste in a plastic bag. Add the oxtails and shake to coat well. In a large soup kettle, melt the butter with the oil. Brown the oxtails, a few at a time, on all sides. Drain on paper towels. Remove and discard excess grease from the pan. Add the onion, leeks, and garlic. Sauté until tender. Return the oxtails to the pan with the veal knuckle, beef stock, tomatoes, purée, bay leaf, Worcestershire, thyme, grated carrot, turnip, barley, and lemon juice. Simmer, covered, for 3 hours. Cool and refrigerate. To finish, remove and discard all surface fat. Remove the meat from the oxtails and discard the bones. Add the onions and carrots. Simmer until tender. Add the wine and cook 5 minutes longer. Discard the bay leaf and veal knuckle. Serve in large bowls piping hot.

SECRETS OF RICH, WELL-FLAVORED, PROPERLY THICKENED STEWS

Coating the meat with a seasoned flour seals in the juices and contributes to a dark brown crustiness. The crusty residue left over from browning adds flavor and color and helps to thicken the stew.

Carefully sauté the meat in a single layer allowing some room between the pieces. Too many pieces at a time lowers the temperature of the shortening in the pan and prevents browning.

Reheat the shortening between browning batches of the meat.

COCK-A-LEEKIE SOUP

PREPARATION: 30 MINUTES
COOKING: 1¼ HOURS
YIELD: 6–8 SERVINGS

1 3-pound frying chicken, cut up
4 cups cold water
4 cups chicken stock
1 cup finely chopped carrots
1 cup finely chopped celery with
    leaves
1 cup finely chopped onion
2 tablespoons chopped fresh parsley
4 whole peppercorns, cracked
1 bay leaf
½ cup pearl barley
2 cups sliced leeks with tender greens
1 cup peeled, diced potato
½ cup dried, pitted prunes, snipped
    into small pieces
1 cup light cream

Each time I ladle out a bowl of delectable Cock-a-Leekie I hear the skirl of the bagpipes proclaiming it Scotland's national soup. It traditionally is served on Robbie Burns Night, when Scots the world over gather to pay tribute to their national poet on his birthday. Steaming tureens of it are paraded in to the accompaniment of a kilted piper's band and sipped with reverence and gusto.

Remove any skin and fat from the chicken. In a large soup kettle, combine the chicken parts, cold water, chicken stock, carrots, celery, onion, parsley, peppercorns, and bay leaf. Cover, and simmer for 45 minutes. Cool the mixture in the broth. Remove the chicken pieces. Discard any skin and bones. Cut the meat into bite-size pieces and return to the pot. Add the barley and simmer for 20 minutes. Stir in the leeks, potato, and snipped prunes. Simmer, uncovered, until tender. Remove and discard the bay leaf. Just before serving, stir in the cream. Heat through but do not boil. Serve at once.

PORTUGUESE CHICKPEA & SAUSAGE SOUP

PREPARATION: OVERNIGHT SOAK-
ING + 25 MINUTES
COOKING: 2½ HOURS
YIELD: 6–8 SERVINGS

2 cups dried chickpeas (garbanzo
　beans)
1 quart cold water
1 pound lean beef, cut into 1-inch
　cubes
2 marrow bones, cracked
6 slices lean bacon, diced
¼ pound Chorizo sausage, sliced thin
3 cups chopped onion
2 cloves garlic, minced
½ cup cubed smoked ham
1 bay leaf
¼ teaspoon coriander seed
¼ teaspoon freshly ground black
　pepper
2 teaspoons chopped fresh mint
1 cup red wine
2 large carrots, sliced thin
2 leeks, sliced with tender greens
4 potatoes, peeled, julienne sliced

*There's an old Portuguese saying, "A soup pot without on-
ions is like a kiss without love!" We concur wholeheartedly.
Chorizo, a zesty Portuguese sausage, usually can be found at
your grocery or specialty store. If not, substitute any spicy,
smoked sausage. This wonderful soup is a meal-in-one.*

Soak the chickpeas overnight in enough water to cover. Drain
and rinse.

In a large soup kettle, simmer the chickpeas and water for 30
minutes. Add the beef and bones. Cover, and simmer slowly for
1½ hours. Skim surface as needed. In a large, heavy skillet, sauté
the bacon until crisp. Remove and drain. Brown the sausage slices
on both sides. Remove and drain. Remove all but 2 tablespoons of
the drippings and discard. Cook the onion and garlic in the remaining fat slowly until tender. Transfer the bacon, sausage, onion, and garlic to the soup kettle. Add the ham, bay leaf, coriander,
black pepper, mint, and wine. Mix well. Simmer, covered, for 30
minutes. Stir in the carrots, leeks, and potatoes. Cook slowly until tender crisp. Season to taste. Remove the bay leaf and bones
and discard. Serve steaming hot in large bowls.

LITHUANIAN MUSHROOM & YOGURT SOUP

PREPARATION: 20 MINUTES
COOKING: 1 HOUR
YIELD: 4–6 SERVINGS

1 tablespoon butter
1 tablespoon vegetable oil
1½ cups finely chopped onion
1 cup finely chopped scallions with
   greens
2 cloves garlic, minced
1 pound fresh mushrooms, cleaned,
   trimmed, and sliced
2 teaspoons Hungarian paprika
3 tablespoons unbleached, all-purpose
   flour
6 cups chicken stock
1 tablespoon fresh lemon juice
1 egg yolk
1½ cups plain yogurt
1 teaspoon chopped fresh dill
¼ teaspoon freshly ground black
   pepper
salt to taste
2 tablespoons chopped fresh chives
fresh dill sprigs

Octogenarians in Lithuania attribute their longevity to eating yogurt and garlic every day. You can heed their example and hope to emulate their accomplishments by serving this delectable, old-world soup often.

In a large soup kettle, melt the butter with the oil. Sauté the onions, scallions, and garlic until tender. Stir in the mushrooms. Cook just until the moisture disappears. Combine the paprika and flour. Sprinkle over the mixture and cook for several minutes. Gradually add the chicken stock and lemon juice. Cook and stir until thickened slightly. Simmer slowly over low heat for 30 minutes, stirring occasionally. Whisk together the egg yolk, yogurt, dill, and pepper. Remove 1 cup of the soup and stir into the yogurt mixture. Mix well and return to the soup. Cook slowly over low heat until thickened. Do not boil. Season to taste. Serve hot, garnished with chopped chives and sprigs of dill.

ONION PATCH SPRING SOUP

PREPARATION: 20 MINUTES
COOKING: 1 HOUR
YIELD: 6–8 SERVINGS

2 tablespoons butter
1 tablespoons olive oil
3 cups sliced sweet onions
2 cups sliced leeks with tender greens
1 cup sliced scallions with greens
¼ cup minced shallots
2 cloves garlic, minced
1 tablespoon unbleached, all-purpose
   flour
8 cups chicken stock
½ cup dry white wine
2 tablespoons fresh lemon juice
salt to taste
freshly ground pepper to taste
2 tablespoons apple brandy
2 tablespoons chopped fresh chives

Giving a recipe your own special touch is one of the delights of cooking. I like to think of Onion Patch Spring Soup as a family get-together with 6 members of the allium clan contributing a share to this production.

In a large soup kettle, melt the butter with the olive oil. Cook the onion slices very slowly over low heat for 20 minutes, until tender and golden. Stir frequently. Add the leeks and scallions. Cook and stir for 5 minutes. Mix in the shallots and garlic. Cook for 3 minutes longer. Do not brown. Sprinkle the flour over the mixture. Stir and cook for 4–5 minutes. Slowly add the stock and wine. Cover and simmer for 20 minutes. Mix in the lemon juice, seasonings to taste, and apple brandy. Simmer for 5 minutes longer. Serve immediately, garnished with chopped chives.

Float minced fresh chives or scallions atop bowls of soup for a brightly accented garnish. Or crumble some french-fried onion rings and scatter over the top of a soup just before serving, for a delightful taste treat.

VICHYSSOISE

PREPARATION: 20 MINUTES
COOKING: 40–50 MINUTES
CHILLING: 4 HOURS
YIELD 4–6 SERVINGS

2 tablespoons butter
1 tablespoon olive oil
4 leeks, finely chopped, white parts
  only
1 cup chopped sweet onion
1 cup chopped celery
4 cups peeled, diced potatoes
4 cups chicken broth
white pepper to taste
1 cup heavy cream
dash nutmeg
¼ cup chopped fresh chives

A classic favorite—the real reason leeks were created. If you're not a chilled soup devotée, this velvety delight can be served hot. Refrigerate first to mingle the flavors, then reheat ever so slowly. Never, ever boil!

In a large, heavy saucepan, melt the butter with the oil. Cook the leeks, onion, and celery slowly over low heat until tender. Do not brown. Stir in the potatoes and chicken broth. Simmer until the potatoes are tender, about 20 minutes. Cool. Purée in a blender or food processor until smooth. Season to taste. Whisk in the cream. Cover and refrigerate for at least 4 hours. To serve, mix gently, dust with nutmeg, and sprinkle with chopped chives.

King Louis XIV of France so feared for his life that he refused to let food pass his lips until it ran the gamut of his Royal Tasters. So exaggerated was the ceremony that by the time the king's favorite leek and potato soup reached the royal table, it was cold. The royal decision? He preferred it that way. Voila! Vichyssoise!

BERMUDA ONION SOUP

PREPARATION: 30 MINUTES
COOKING: 1¾ HOURS
YIELD: 6–8 SERVINGS

2 tablespoons butter
2 tablespoons vegetable oil
8 cups thinly sliced sweet onions
½ teaspoon dry mustard
2 teaspoons sugar
3 tablespoons unbleached, all-purpose
  flour
2 quarts beef stock
¼ teaspoon freshly ground black
  pepper
1 bay leaf
1 cup dry white wine
4 tablespoons chopped fresh parsley
6 slices day-old crusty bread, ½ inch
  thick
2 cups grated Swiss cheese
chopped fresh chives

Bermudians contend that a simmering kettle of onion soup sings of a happy home. For certain, it beckons one and all to the table with its aromatic fragrance and embodies the spirit of onion cookery. Ensure success by using a rich, full-bodied beef stock. Cook the onions long and slowly to release their full, sweet flavor and heighten their color to a deep gold.

In a large, heavy skillet, melt the butter with the oil. Separate the onion slices into rings. Cook very slowly over low heat for 45 minutes, until golden. Mix the dry mustard, sugar, and flour. Sprinkle the flour mixture over the onion and cook for several minutes. Stir in 1 cup of beef stock to deglaze the pan. Transfer the mixture to a large soup kettle. Add the remaining beef stock, pepper, bay leaf, wine, and parsley. Simmer and stir, covered, over low heat for 1 hour. Remove and discard the bay leaf. Toast the bread slices until crisp. Butter on both sides. Sprinkle with the grated cheese on one side. Broil the slices lightly until the cheese is melted and golden. Ladle the soup into deep bowls. Float a slice of toast in each bowl with the cheese-side up. Sprinkle with chopped chives. Serve immediately.

VARIATIONS

PORTUGUESE ONION SOUP OPORTO WITH POACHED EGGS.
Ladle the onion soup into six ovenproof soup crocks. Add 1 teaspoon of port or Madeira wine to each crock. Float the toasted bread slices on top of the soup. Place 1 drained, poached egg on top of each slice of toast. Serve immediately.

WHOLE ONION SOUP WITH PUFF PASTRY CAP. Preheat oven to 375°F. Cook 6 small onions in their skins until tender. Cool. Remove and discard the skins. Trim the bottoms to allow each onion to stand. Cut a thin slice from the top of each onion. Make an X across the top to keep the center intact. Place 1 onion in each of six ovenproof soup crocks. Fill with hot onion soup. Sprinkle generously with grated cheese. Defrost 1 package of puff pastry shells. Roll out each shell to a 7-inch circle. Dampen the edges with water. Place 1 pastry circle over the top of each soup crock. Press firmly to the sides and crimp the edges. Brush the tops with beaten egg. Make two tiny slits in the top for steam to escape. Bake about 20 minutes, until soup is heated through and the pastry is puffed and golden. Serve immediately.

CREAM OF ONION SOUP. In a blender or food processor, blend 1 3-ounce package of cream cheese with ½ cup milk and ½ cup cream. Slowly add the mixture to the onion soup, stirring constantly. Heat through and serve at once.

BARE BONES TURKEY CHOWDER WITH CHIVE DUMPLINGS

PREPARATION: 25 MINUTES
COOKING: 3 HOURS
YIELD: 6–8 SERVINGS

1 meaty turkey carcass, cut apart
8 cups cold water
1 bay leaf
4 cups chopped onion
3 cups chicken stock
2 cups shredded cabbage
1 clove garlic, minced
1½ cups chopped celery, including
    tops
1 large potato, peeled and diced
1½ cups corn kernels
1½ cups sliced carrots
1 cup green beans, sliced
12 1-inch pearl onions, peeled
1 cup chopped fresh spinach leaves
2 tomatoes, peeled and coarsely
    chopped
½ cup chopped fresh parsley
salt to taste
¼ teaspoon freshly ground black
    pepper
1 teaspoon dried basil
Chive Dumplings (see next page)

Affectionately referred to as "Play it again, Tom!", this old family favorite makes an appearance on the menu once the holiday bird approaches the skeleton stage. Besides a goodly pinch of kitchen thrift, recipe ingredients can include whatever leftovers the refrigerator yields. Just don't spare the onions—the more, the better.

In a large soup kettle, combine the turkey carcass, water, bay leaf, and onions. Simmer, covered, for 2 hours. Remove the carcass, cool, and pull off any meat. Discard the bones. Chop and return the meat to the pot. Add the remaining ingredients, except the dumplings. Simmer slowly for 45 minutes or until the vegetables are tender. Remove and discard the bay leaf. Drop the dumplings into the simmering chowder. Cover tightly and simmer for 20 minutes without raising the lid. Serve piping hot.

CHIVE DUMPLINGS

PREPARATION: 10 MINUTES   COOKING: 20 MINUTES   YIELD: 6 DUMPLINGS

1½ cups unbleached, all-purpose flour
2 teaspoons baking powder
½ teaspoon salt
2 tablespoons chopped fresh parsley
3 tablespoons chopped fresh chives
3 tablespoons vegetable shortening
½ cup milk

Sift together the flour, baking powder, and salt. Mix in the parsley and chives. Cut in the shortening until the mixture resembles coarse meal. Add only enough milk to hold the dough together. Drop spoonfuls of the dough on top of bubbling soup. Cover and simmer for 20 minutes without lifting the cover.

Dumplings need a soup with lots of broth, and they don't like to be crowded. Drop each dumpling gently into the bubbling liquid. Stir carefully so the dumplings don't stick to the bottom of the pan. Once they float to the top, cover the pan. Do not lift the lid! If curiosity tends to get the better of you, use a glass lid or invert a glass pie plate over the top of the soup kettle for viewing. Be sure to steam-simmer dumplings—do not boil!

KNOCK-YOUR-SOCKS-OFF CHILI

PREPARATION: 25 MINUTES
COOKING: 2 HOURS
YIELD: 6–8 SERVINGS

2 pounds lean ground beef
1 pound lean pork, cut into ½-inch
  cubes
4 cups coarsely chopped onion
3 cloves garlic, minced
1 cup chopped green bell pepper
3 tablespoons chili powder (or to
  taste)
½ cup beer
4 cups tomato purée
¾ cup tomato paste
4 ripe tomatoes, peeled and coarsely
  chopped
1 teaspoon ground cumin
1 bay leaf
½ teaspoon freshly ground black
  pepper
1 teaspoon oregano
4 cups cooked red kidney beans
1 cup shredded cheese
2 flour tortillas, cut into wedges

Folks up North consider this a chili with personality. Westerners may deem it a little on the tame side and perk it up with additional chili powder or jalapeno peppers. Whatever the taste preference—spicy, spicier or spiciest—it's an all-time favorite.

Brown the beef and pork in a large soup kettle. Stir in the onions, garlic, and green pepper. Cook until tender. Add the chili powder, beer, tomato purée and paste, chopped tomatoes, cumin, bay leaf, black pepper, and oregano. Mix well. Simmer slowly for 1½ hours, stirring occasionally. Add the kidney beans and cook 30 minutes longer. Remove and discard the bay leaf. Ladle the chili into bowls. Sprinkle generously with the shredded cheese. Serve piping hot with tortilla wedges.

STORMY WEATHER FISH CHOWDER

PREPARATION: 25 MINUTES
COOKING: 50–60 MINUTES
YIELD: 6–8 SERVINGS

6 slices lean bacon, diced
2 pounds white fish fillets, cut into
   bite-size pieces
2 cups chopped Bermuda onions
½ cup chopped green pepper
1 clove garlic, minced
2 tablespoons fresh lemon juice
4 cups fish stock or bottled clam juice
1 small onion, stuck with 2 whole
   cloves
1 teaspoon grated lemon rind
1 bay leaf
2 tablespoons chopped fresh dill
1 cup chopped, peeled tomatoes
1 cup chopped carrots
2 potatoes, peeled and diced
¼ cup chopped fresh parsley
1 teaspoon Worcestershire sauce
1 cup cream
½ cup dark rum
Sprigs of fresh dill

Atlantic gales have a way of whetting the appetite and bringing out the soup kettle in Bermuda. An island favorite, this time-honored recipe calls for fresh dill, an aromatic herb that grows in feathery profusion all over the Atlantic paradise. Native Bermudians regale visitors with tales of how the fish jump out of the ocean right into the pot. However they get there, the end result is sensational.

In a large soup kettle, sauté the bacon until crisp. Remove, drain, and set aside. Pat the fish pieces dry. Over high heat, sauté the fish pieces quickly until golden. Remove and reserve. Sauté the onions, green peppers, and garlic until tender. Stir in the lemon juice, fish stock, onion with cloves, lemon rind, bay leaf, dill, tomatoes, carrots, potatoes, parsley, and Worcestershire sauce. Simmer just until the vegetables are tender, 15–20 minutes. Stir in the fish pieces, cream, and rum. Reheat just until hot, do not boil. Ladle into bowls and garnish with crumbled bacon and dill sprigs.

SCOTCH BROTH MACGREGOR WITH OATMEAL DUMPLINGS

PREPARATION: 30 MINUTES
COOKING: 3½ HOURS
YIELD: 6–8 SERVINGS

2 quarts cold water
3 pounds lean, meaty lamb bones,
　　cracked
½ cup pearl barley
1 bay leaf
2 tablespoons chopped fresh parsley
1 teaspoon thyme
onion peel from 2 onions, washed
2 cups coarsely chopped onion
2 leeks, sliced with tender greens
1 cup chopped carrots
1 cup chopped turnip
1 cup sliced celery with greens
1 clove garlic, peeled and halved
1 cup fresh peas
¼ teaspoon freshly ground black
　　pepper
Oatmeal Dumplings (see next page)

This soup claims its birthright high in the heathered hills of Scotland, and any good Scotch cook will gladly part with a word of advice when asked about making it. "Dinna lift the lid once you've plopped in the dumplings!" Keep the pot simmering, everyone's sure to want a wee bit more.

In a large soup kettle, combine the water, lamb bones, barley, bay leaf, parsley, thyme, and onion peel (it adds a rich color to the broth). Simmer, covered, for 2 hours. Stir and skim occasionally. Remove and discard the onion skins. Stir in the chopped onions, leeks, carrots, turnip, celery, and garlic. Simmer, covered, for 1 hour. Remove the bones and cut the meat into bite-size pieces. Discard the bones. Return the meat to the pot. Add the peas and pepper. Bring to a boil. Drop in the dumplings. Reduce the heat, cover tightly, and simmer for 20 minutes. Remove and discard the bay leaf. Serve piping hot with one or two dumplings per serving.

NOTE: For less fatty soup, chill the soup before adding the dumplings. Skim off the fat and reheat to boiling. Proceed as directed. When refrigerating any leftover soup, separate the dumplings and store in another container.

OATMEAL DUMPLINGS

PREPARATION: 10 MINUTES　　　　COOKING: 20 MINUTES　　　　YIELD: 8 DUMPLINGS

1½ cups unbleached, all-purpose flour
1 teaspoon baking powder
1 cup regular rolled oats (not quick-cooking)
1 tablespoon chopped fresh parsley
3 tablespoons vegetable shortening
½ cup milk
1 tablespoon grated onion

Sift together the flour and baking powder. Stir in the oatmeal and parsley. Cut in 3 tablespoons shortening until the mixture resembles coarse meal. Mix the milk and grated onion. Stir into the oatmeal mixture until just blended. If too dry, add enough milk to make a soft dough. Drop by tablespoonfuls into soup or stew.

ONIONS ALONE

AN ONION BELIEVES wholeheartedly in its own importance. Once considered among the lowliest of vegetables, it has risen through the ranks to take its place among the elite of garden royalty. Long respected as a cook's best friend, onions add flavor, fragrance, texture, and variety to countless recipes. When you feature an onion as the solo performer, it needs little introduction and captivates audiences with its ability to hold its own center stage.

Consider the onion's versatility. You can bake, boil, braise, broil, deep fry, grill, microwave, pickle, pressure cook, roast, sauté, scallop, steam, stew, stir fry, and eat an onion raw. No other vegetable can claim this unique distinction.

According to the U.S. Department of Agriculture, onions are right up there on the popularity charts. They rate among the ten most favorite vegetables in the United States. Collectively, alliums are low in calories and a boon to weight watchers fighting the battle of the bulge. When it comes to supplying essential vitamins, minerals, carbohydrates, and fiber to our diets, they pack a real wallop. They make a major contribution to the health and well being of our bodies, by promoting good digestion.

We heartily recommend them on the economic front. Deliciously filling and so gentle to a battered budget, onion recipes stretch the food dollar to the point of elasticity.

Discover what gourmet cooks such as Brillat-Savarin, Soubise, Bechamel, and Beard have known only too well as they savored the sweet, oniony smell of success. Alliums should be prized and used to create superb dishes—not relegated to insignificance in the vegetable bin.

THE BASICS

The thought of onionless cooking sends chills up and down my spine. A famous French chef once philosophized, "Where would civilization be without onions?" Where, indeed? Cooks in every corner of the globe reach for them almost as automatically as they reach for their favorite pots and pans.

Here are some of the basics to help you "know your onions."

BOILED ONIONS—Small onions, ½–2 inches, are best for boiling whole. Blanch and peel white or silverskin onions. Leave the root end intact during cooking. Make a small X in the top of each onion to prevent the center from popping out. Cover with water and add a dash of lemon juice or vinegar to preserve the whiteness. Dry white wine or chicken or beef stock can be substituted. Simmer, covered, until tender crisp, 10–15 minutes. Drain and season to taste. Reserve the stock for soup.

PARBOILED ONIONS—When the onions are needed for another recipe, prepare as above but reduce the cooking time to 8 minutes. Omit the seasoning.

STEAMED ONIONS—Wash but do not peel the onions. Place them on a rack, steamer, or colander over 1 inch of boiling water. Steam until tender, about 30 minutes. Maintain the water level while steaming. Drain, cool, and peel.

CREAMED ONIONS—Cook 12–15 small white or silverskin onions by boiling or steaming. Do not season. In a large saucepan, melt 3 tablespoons butter. Blend in 2 tablespoons unbleached, all-purpose flour. Cook and stir for 3 minutes. Remove from the heat. Combine 1½ cups warm milk with ½ cup warm cream. Stir into the flour mixture. Whisk for 5 minutes over low heat until thick and smooth. Add the onions and 2 tablespoons chopped fresh parsley. Heat through but do not boil. Season to taste. Sprinkle with freshly grated nutmeg or Hungarian paprika.

But lest your kissing should be spoiled, your onions must be thoroughly boiled.
—Jonathan Swift

CHEDDARED ONIONS—Prepare Creamed Onions. Stir in 1 cup of grated, sharp Cheddar cheese until melted, before garnishing. Serve immediately.

SHERRIED ONIONS—Prepare Creamed Onions. Stir in 2 tablespoons dry sherry just before serving.

GLAZED ONIONS—Blanch, peel, trim, and make an X in top of small white or silverskin onions. Place in a large, heavy sauté pan big enough to hold the onions in one layer. Cover halfway with water. Add 1 tablespoon butter and ½ teaspoon sugar. Simmer, covered, over low heat. Shake the pan occasionally to prevent sticking. After 15 minutes remove the lid. Increase the heat and cook just until the water evaporates. Shake the pan constantly to prevent browning or scorching. Cook just until the onions are covered with a shiny, white glaze.

GOLDEN HONEY-GLAZED ONIONS—Blanch, peel, trim, and make an X in top of 12–15 small white or silverskin onions. In a large saucepan, cover the onions with rich beef stock and simmer until tender crisp, about 15 minutes. Do not overcook. Cool the onions in the stock. Drain and pat dry. Reserve the stock for soup. In a large, heavy skillet, melt 3 tablespoons butter with 2 tablespoons vegetable oil over low heat. Stir in ½ cup honey and 4 tablespoons fresh lemon juice. Add the onions, stirring constantly to coat thoroughly. Cook slowly over very low heat, 20–30 minutes. Stir gently and shake the pan constantly to prevent scorching. Don't be distracted, as onions burn easily. Cook until coppery gold. Season to taste. Serve as a vegetable or as a garnish for roasts and fowl.

OVEN-BAKED GLAZED ONIONS—Prepare onions for cooking as above. Arrange the onions in one layer in a buttered baking dish. Combine 4 tablespoons melted butter, 2 tablespoons honey, and 3 tablespoons fresh lemon juice. Pour over the onions to coat thor-

Come follow me by the smell. Here are delicate onions to sell. I promise to use you well. They make the blood warmer. You'll feed like a farmer.
—Jonathan Swift

oughly. Bake in a preheated 350°F oven for 30 minutes, or until tender and golden brown. Baste frequently.

BARBECUED WHOLE ONIONS—Blanch, peel, trim, and make an X in top of 12–15 small white or silverskin onions. Arrange in one layer in greased baking dish. Pour ¹ cup of *Bourbon Barbecue Sauce* (page 148) over onions. Toss lightly to coat. Bake in a preheated 350°F oven for 30 minutes, or until tender. Baste frequently. Serve bubbling hot as a vegetable or garnish for grilled steak or chicken.

OVEN-ROASTED ONIONS—Peel, trim, and make an X in top of medium-size onions. Place in the roasting pan, surrounding roast, 45 minutes before the end of cooking time. Turn the onions to brown evenly. Baste frequently with pan juices.

BAKED ONIONS—Wash but do not peel medium-size onions. Trim the bottoms slightly to allow them to stand up in a casserole dish in one layer. Cover the bottom of the dish with enough water to prevent scorching. Bake for 1½ hours in preheated 350°F oven until soft to the touch. Remove and cool. Cut a slice from the root end and peel. Top each onion with butter and a sprinkling of chopped fresh parsley. Season to taste. Serve at once.

SAUTÉED ONIONS—Slice or chop peeled onions. Heat a large, heavy skillet and sauté the onions in butter and oil quickly over even heat until limp and translucent. Do not brown. Stir constantly to prevent scorching.

PAN-FRIED ONIONS—Prepare as for Sautéed Onions. Cook slowly over low heat until golden. Do not brown. Stir constantly.

STEAM-SAUTÉED ONIONS—Substitute stock, water, or wine (or a combination) for the butter and oil in Sautéed Onions. Cover the bottom of skillet (not cast-iron) about ⅛ inch deep. Bring to a boil, add onions, leeks, shallots, or garlic to be "sautéed." Cover

> Deglazing the pan after sautéing is the secret to a better-tasting soup or stew. Add some liquid to the pan, scrape up the rich residue that remains, and combine with the remaining ingredients.

and reduce heat. Stir constantly, adding more liquid as needed, until cooked to desired doneness.

SAUTÉED WHOLE ONION SLICES—Peel and cut 2 large onions into ½-inch-thick slices. Keep intact. Arrange in a large, heavy skillet (not cast-iron). Do not crowd. Pour in ¼ cup stock, water, or wine. Steam until tender crisp. Drain off excess cooking liquid while holding slices together with a large spatula. Add butter and oil. Heat to sizzling and sauté the slices until golden on both sides.

BROILED WHOLE ONION SLICES—Peel and cut large onions into ½-inch-thick slices. Keep intact. Arrange in a shallow baking pan in one layer. Sprinkle with ¼ cup boiling water or stock. Bake for 15 minutes in a preheated 350°F oven. Remove carefully with slotted spatula. Drain and arrange on oven broiler pan. Brush with melted butter. Season to taste. Broil on both sides until golden.

OVEN-BAKED ONION SLICES—Prepare as for Broiled Onion Slices. Brush with melted butter. Omit the broiling.

OVEN-BAKED ONION SLICES WITH SHERRIED CREAM—Prepare as for Broiled Onion Slices. Substitute chicken stock for water. When the onion slices are tender crisp, combine ¾ cup light cream with 4 tablespoons dry sherry. Pour over the slices. Dot with butter, cover, and bake for 15 minutes longer or until golden.

ONION PURÉE—Cook 2 cups of peeled, chopped onions in 2 cups of chicken stock until tender. Cool and purée in a blender or food processor. In a medium saucepan, melt 3 tablespoons butter. Blend in 2 tablespoons unbleached, all-purpose flour. Cook over low heat for 5 minutes. Stir in the onion purée and blend well. Season to taste. Use as a base for soups and gravies.

CHARCOAL-GRILLED WHOLE ONIONS—Brush unpeeled onions with oil. Place in hot coals. Turn frequently until inside is soft when

The sliced onions give of their essence after a brew and become the ambrosia for gods and men.
—Jane Bothwell

So enamored of leek soup was the Roman emperor Nero that his subjects christened him "Porrophagus," from the Latin name for leek, *porrum*. This passion rated second only to his love for playing the violin.

Well loved he garleek, oynons, and eek lekes,
And for to drynken strong wyn, reed as blood.
—Geoffrey Chaucer

squeezed. Remove the charred outer layers. Season to taste and serve.

BOILED LEEKS—Trim off the shaggy root hair and remove damaged upper green leaves from 3–4 medium-size leeks. Leave 2–2½ inches of tender greens. Slit open the leeks and wash thoroughly under running water to remove the grit and sand. Drain. Place in a large skillet. Cover with 1 cup water or chicken or beef broth. Simmer for 12–15 minutes, or until tender crisp. Drain well. Season to taste. Add butter and serve at once.

SAUTÉED LEEKS—Prepare as for Boiled Leeks. Slice into thin rings. In a large skillet, melt 1 tablespoon butter with 1 tablespoon vegetable oil. Sauté until tender crisp. Season to taste.

STEAMED-SAUTÉED LEEKS—Prepare as for Sautéed Leeks. Omit the butter and oil. In a sauté pan, bring to a boil ½ cup water, stock, or dry white wine. Add the sliced leeks and cook until tender crisp. Season to taste.

SAUTÉED WHOLE SCALLIONS—Wash and trim 8–10 scallions. Leave 3–4 inches of greens. In a sauté pan, heat ½ cup water or stock with 2 tablespoons butter. Cook the scallions until tender crisp, about 4–5 minutes. Drain well. Season to taste.

SAUTÉED CHOPPED SCALLIONS—Wash and trim scallions. Leave 3–4 inches of greens. Chop into small pieces. Melt butter with oil in a skillet. Sauté the scallions until tender crisp. Season to taste.

SAUTÉED SHALLOTS—Peel and dice desired amount of shallots. Melt butter with oil in a skillet. Sauté until tender crisp. Do not brown shallots, or they will become bitter.

SAUTÉED GARLIC—Peel and mince the garlic. Melt butter with oil in skillet. Sauté until tender. Do not brown garlic, or it will become bitter.

GARLIC PURÉE—Prepare *Baked Garlic Spread*, page 39. Substitute 2 tablespoons olive oil for the butter. Purée in a blender or food processor until smooth or press through a sieve and add the olive oil. Store in a jar with a tight-fitting cover. Pour a thin film of olive oil on top of the purée. Store in the refrigerator. Use the mixture as a flavoring in dressings, sauces, vegetable dishes, and with meat and poultry.

STUFFED ONIONS

There were ruddy, brown-girthed Spanish onions, shining in the fatness of their growth like a Spanish friar.
—Charles Dickens

Onions are for stuffing! Heap them high with a succulent filling and top with a savory sauce. They become epicurean delights. An onion's size, shape, and texture make an ideal casing into which an unending variety of fillings can be popped. Everything from leftovers to gourmet delicacies finds a welcome haven in hollowed-out onion shells. Bake them ever so slowly in a rich stock to develop a mild, sweet flavor that permeates both stuffing and cooking liquid.

Select large, firm, symmetrical onions for stuffing. I prefer the sweet Bermuda or Spanish onion. Don't be tempted into substituting older, sprouted onions for economy's sake. Remember—the fresher and firmer the onion, the better the finished product.

To prepare for stuffing, blanch the peeled onions in boiling water for 15 minutes. Remove, cool, and drain well. To create a flat base for each onion to rest on, trim a thin piece off the root end. Cut a thin slice off the top of each onion. Hollow out the onion center to form a solid shell ¼ inch thick. Do not cut through the bottom. I use a pointed, serrated grapefruit spoon—it works beautifully. Chop the scooped-out centers and reserve.

These stuffings will fill 4 medium-size onions. To stuff, sauté the chopped centers in butter and oil until tender crisp. Mix with any one of the following stuffings:

CARROT—½ cup cooked chopped carrots, ¼ cup cooked chopped celery, ½ cup grated cheese, and ½ cup cooked rice.

CORN—1 cup drained, whole corn kernels, 1 tablespoon chopped fresh parsley, ½ cup soft wholewheat breadcrumbs, and 2 tablespoons melted butter.

NUTS—½ cup chopped nuts, ½ cup cooked brown rice, ½ cup skinned and chopped tomatoes, and ¼ teaspoon oregano.

CHEESE—½ cup grated Swiss cheese, ½ cup cooked brown rice, ¼ cup soft wholewheat breadcrumbs, and 2 tablespoons milk mixed with ¼ teaspoon dry mustard.

SAUSAGE—1 cup cooked, crumbled pork or Italian sausage, ½ cup soft breadcrumbs, ¼ cup chopped almonds, 1 tablespoon chopped fresh parsley, and 2 or more tablespoons chicken stock or wine.

SHRIMP—1 cup finely diced, cooked shrimp, ½ cup crushed crackers, ½ cup chopped, cooked mushrooms, 1 tablespoon chopped fresh parsley, 2 tablespoons cream, and a dash of curry.

HAM—½ cup finely diced, cooked ham, 1 cup diced, cooked chestnuts, ½ cup cooked wild rice, 1 tablespoon melted butter, and 1 tablespoon crumbled blue cheese.

LIVER—¼ pound cooked, chopped chicken livers, 2 strips cooked, crumbled bacon, ¼ cup chopped pistachio nuts, and 2 tablespoons sour cream.

To cook, first **preheat the oven to 400°F**. Spoon the stuffing into the onion shells. Heap ½ inch over the top of the rim. Do not pack down. Place the stuffed onions in a shallow baking dish to hold them snugly. Pour a mixture of ½ wine and ½ beef stock to reach halfway up the onions. Sprinkle the onions with buttered breadcrumbs. Cover the dish loosely with foil. Bake for 15 minutes. Remove the foil. Reduce the heat to 350°F and cook until the tops are golden and the liquid begins to thicken, about 20–25 minutes. Baste the onions frequently to keep them moist. Drain and serve immediately.

NOTE: Give leftovers and your budget a new lease on life by tucking yesterday's goodies into onion shells. Use any one of the following: chili, beef stew, macaroni and cheese, Spanish rice, poultry stuffing, sauerkraut (for the valiant only), tuna and rice, ground ham, or corned beef hash. Let your imagination be your guide!

FRENCH-FRIED ONION RINGS IN BEER BATTER

PREPARATION: 30 MINUTES
STANDING: 1 HOUR
COOKING: 3–5 MINUTES/BATCH
YIELD: 4 SERVINGS

2 cups unbleached, all-purpose flour
¼ teaspoon freshly ground black
   pepper
salt to taste
2 eggs, separated
1 cup (8 ounces) beer
¼ cup melted butter
3 sweet onions

Deep fried to golden perfection, french-fried onion rings are an all-American favorite with their crunchy outer layers and moist succulent centers. Beer batter makes them taste even better. Pile the plates high and make enough. Seconds are inevitable.

In a large bowl, sift together the flour, pepper, and salt to taste. Whisk the egg yolks until light and lemony. Add the beer and butter. Mix well. Gradually stir in the flour until well blended. Let stand at room temperature for 1 hour. Beat the egg whites until stiff. Gently fold into the batter. Heat the oil to 375°F and keep constant while cooking.

Peel and slice the onions into ¼-inch rounds. Separate into rings. Coat each ring with flour. Dip, one at a time, into the batter. Drain off any excess. Cook, several at a time, until golden. Turn to cook evenly. Do not crowd. Drain on paper towels. Keep warm on a baking sheet lined with paper towels in a 200°F oven until all the rings are cooked. Serve at once.

FRENCH-FRIED ONION FACTS

- I prefer peanut oil for deep frying. Its smoking point is higher than most fats; it stores well; and its flavor does not overwhelm the star attraction.
- Always drain onion rings on paper towels. Blot up the last traces of fat before serving.
- Serve crisp onion rings on a separate plate to avoid absorbing liquids from other foods.
- Never, never cover onion rings to keep them warm. You will end up with a limp, soggy heap of unpalatable onions.

Onions & Friends

Two rivers on separate continents were named for the profusion of wild onions growing along their banks—the Winooski River in Vermont, USA, (*winooski* is an Abnaki Indian word meaning "wild onion"), and L'Oignon in Burgundy, France.

A SIDE DISH OF GARDEN DELIGHTS is always welcome at the table. No matter what the menu, it's easy to balance flavor, color, and nutrition with a lively mix of vegetables.

Onions are born mixers. Blessed with compatibility, they live on intimate terms with their fellow vegetables. Each member of the onion family possesses chameleon characteristics and a built-in ability to dramatize any dish into which it is grated, chopped, sliced, or plopped whole.

Depending on their involvement, alliums can be flamboyant or subdued. They tantalize the senses as they simmer subtly in Brazilian Black Beans in Rum or shout from the stovetop, "I'm for supper!" when sizzling in Onion Medley Stir Fry.

There is something absolutely wonderful about the marriage of onions and potatoes. It certainly eliminates that old mealtime bugaboo—potato predictability.

The delectable combination of creamy mashed potatoes and leeks, christened Colcannon by the Irish, has sustained them for centuries. There isn't a Frenchman alive who wouldn't smack his lips with an emotional "Magnifique!" for Onion and Potato Parisienne. Simmered long and slowly to creamy perfection, this crusty, golden gratin is not to be denied. Wafer-thin onion rings, broiled to a golden crispness and spiraled around mashed potato puffs, lend a regal air to any meat, fowl, or fish entrée. I am ecstatically content to eat them all by themselves.

It's time to get off the vegetable treadmill. Take advantage of whatever bounty the garden yields, or bargains the supermarket offers, to transform vegetables into deliciously different eating.

ONION & EGGPLANT CASSEROLE WITH LENTILS

PREPARATION: 25 MINUTES
BAKING: 20–25 MINUTES
YIELD: 4 SERVINGS

3 tablespoons butter
1 tablespoon vegetable oil
4 cups pared and cubed eggplant (1 pound)
1 cup chopped onion
1 cup sliced celery
¼ cup chopped green pepper
1 cup stewed tomatoes
2 cups cooked lentils, drained
salt and freshly ground pepper to taste
1 cup grated Cheddar cheese
1½ cups coarsely crushed corn chips

Don't discount the lowly lentil. Teamed with eggplant, onions and cheese, it makes for delicious, nutritious eating. Crushed corn-chips.lend a crunchy texture to this savory casserole.

Preheat oven to 350°F. In a large, heavy skillet, melt the butter with oil. Cook and stir the eggplant, onion, celery, and green pepper until tender crisp. Mix in the tomatoes, lentils, and salt and pepper to taste. Add ½ cup Cheddar cheese and 1 cup corn chips. Mix well. Turn into a greased baking dish. Combine the remaining cheese and corn chips. Sprinkle over the top. Bake 20–25 minutes, until the top is golden. Serve immediately.

BRAZILIAN BLACK BEANS IN RUM

PREPARATION: 15 MINUTES
SOAKING: 1 HOUR
COOKING: 2 HOURS, 40 MINUTES
YIELD: 6–8 SERVINGS

½ pound dried black beans
4 cups water
1 small onion, peeled and studded
   with 4 cloves
1 clove garlic, peeled
1 bay leaf
2 tablespoons chopped fresh parsley
1 tablespoon butter
1 tablespoon vegetable oil
2 cups chopped onion
½ cup chopped green pepper
3 tomatoes, chopped
1 clove garlic, minced
4 slices cooked bacon, crumbled
2 teaspoons dry mustard
½ cup molasses
pinch cayenne pepper
½ cup dark rum
1 cup sour cream

Cooked the spicy, South American way, this traditional dish exudes personality. Adjust the seasonings to suit your taste buds—meek, mild, or adventurous. Simmer the beans slowly, then spike with rum just before serving. Age improves this recipe, so make it ahead and reheat when ready to serve.

In a large soup kettle, boil the beans and water for 2 minutes. Remove from the heat, cover, and let stand for 1 hour. Add the clove-studded onion, clove of garlic, bay leaf, and parsley. Cover and simmer for 2 hours. Remove onion, garlic, and bay leaf. In a large skillet, melt the butter with the oil. Sauté the onion, green pepper, tomatoes, and minced garlic until tender. Stir in the bacon, mustard, molasses, cayenne pepper, and half of the rum. Mix well. Transfer the mixture to a bean pot or casserole dish. Cover and bake at 350°F until tender and bubbly. Just before serving, pour the remaining rum over the beans. Dollop each serving with sour cream and serve piping hot.

APPLE 'N ONION STUFFED ACORN SQUASH

PREPARATION: 30 MINUTES
BAKING: 15–20 MINUTES
YIELD: 4 SERVINGS

½ cup seedless raisins
¼ cup red wine
2 large acorn squashes
1 tablespoon butter
1 tablespoon vegetable oil
1 cup chopped onion
1 clove garlic, minced
1 red apple, peeled, cored, and
   chopped
2 tablespoons honey
dash curry (optional)
2 slices wholewheat bread, crumbled
½ cup cooked brown rice
¼ teaspoon freshly ground black
   pepper
½ cup chopped walnuts

When it comes to stuffing squash, it's impossible to over-state the virtues of this recipe. Onions, apples, wine-soaked raisins, and crunchy brown rice add new taste dimensions. It's as delicious as it is healthy to eat.

Preheat oven to 375°F. In a small bowl, marinate the raisins in the wine. Halve the squashes lengthwise and remove the seeds. Place the cut sides down in a shallow baking dish. Add a small amount of water to prevent scorching. Bake in a 375°F oven for 20 minutes. Meanwhile, melt the butter with the oil in a large, heavy skillet. Cook the onions slowly until tender and golden. Add the garlic and apple. Cook and stir for 5 minutes longer. Stir in the honey and curry. Combine the bread, rice, raisins, and wine. Mix into the onions. Remove the squash from the oven. Turn right side up. Drain any water from the baking dish. Spoon the stuffing mixture into each hollow. Sprinkle with pepper and walnuts. Bake until squash is tender, 15–20 minutes. Serve immediately.

COLCANNON

PREPARATION: 25 MINUTES
BAKING: 15–20 MINUTES
YIELD: 8 SERVINGS

4 cups hot mashed potatoes
3 cups coarsely shredded green
  cabbage
2 leeks, trimmed, washed, and thinly
  sliced (include 1 inch of tender
  greens)
½ cup milk, warmed
6 tablespoons butter
salt to taste
½ teaspoon freshly ground black
  pepper
2 tablespoons chopped fresh parsley

Some would have you believe that this dish from the Emerald Isle was born of Saturday night's leftovers. Not so! Pure and simple, it reflects the Irish love for potatoes, onions, and cabbage. Not necessarily in that order. And 'tis cursed you'll be if you use packaged instant potatoes.

Preheat oven to 400°F. Keep the mashed potatoes warm. In a large skillet, steam-sauté the cabbage and leeks in a small amount of boiling water until tender. Drain well. Using a fork, beat the mashed potatoes until light and fluffy. Stir in the milk, 4 tablespoons of butter, salt and pepper. Mix well. Add the well-drained cabbage and leeks. Spoon into a buttered casserole dish. Bake for 15 minutes or until the top is golden brown. Remove and make a depression in the center. Fill with the remaining 2 tablespoons butter. Garnish with chopped parsley. Serve piping hot.

VARIATION

Omit the cabbage and leeks. Instead, steam-sauté 2 cups of chopped scallions. This version is sometimes called "Champ."

HOPPIN' JOHN

PREPARATION: 10 MINUTES PLUS 1
HOUR SOAKING TIME
COOKING: 1½ HOURS
YIELD: 6–8 SERVINGS

1 pound (2 cups) dried black-eyed
  peas
6 cups water
1 meaty ham bone
2 cups chopped onion
1 cup chopped celery, including tops
1 bay leaf
1 clove garlic, minced
¼ teaspoon freshly ground black
  pepper
¼ teaspoon crushed, dried red pepper
2 tablespoons chopped fresh parsley
1 cup uncooked wild or long grain rice

Brought to the new world centuries ago by African slaves, this delicacy of black-eyed peas and ham traditionally is eaten on New Year's Day to assure good luck throughout the year. But don't wait until January 1 to enjoy it.

Combine the peas with the water in a large soup kettle. Boil for two minutes. Remove from the heat and let stand for one hour. Add the ham bone, onion, celery, bay leaf, garlic, black and red pepper, and parsley. Cover and simmer for 45 minutes. Stir in the rice. Cover tightly and simmer until peas and rice are tender, about 45 minutes. Remove the ham bone. Dice the remaining ham and return to the pan. Discard the bone. Remove and discard the bay leaf. Reheat and serve immediately with a cruet of vinegar for sprinkling.

ONION MEDLEY STIR FRY

PREPARATION: 15 MINUTES
COOKING: 5 MINUTES
YIELD: 6 SERVINGS

½ cup orange juice
1 tablespoon soy sauce
2 teaspoons cornstarch
1 teaspoon minced fresh ginger root
    or ¼ teaspoon ground ginger
1 tablespoon sesame oil
1 tablespoon vegetable oil
2 sweet onions, thinly sliced
1 cup finely sliced celery
2 cloves garlic, minced
1 small green pepper, halved, seeded,
    and cut into thin strips
1 small red pepper, halved, seeded,
    and cut into thin strips

Stir fry means just that—keep stirring! Serve this quick-to-fix combination with its bright colors and crisp texture often.

Whisk together the orange juice, soy sauce, cornstarch, and ginger. Set aside. In a large sauté pan or wok, heat the oils. Using high heat, stir fry the onions, celery, and garlic for 2 minutes. Add the green and red pepper strips. Stir fry until tender crisp, 2–3 minutes. Quickly stir in the orange sauce. Heat through and serve immediately.

SWEET & SOUR CABBAGE COMBO

PREPARATION: 20 MINUTES
COOKING: 40–50 MINUTES
YIELD: 4 SERVINGS

4 slices bacon, diced
1½ cups finely chopped onion
4 cups shredded red cabbage
2 tart apples, peeled, cored, and thinly
 sliced
1 cup apple cider
3 tablespoons cider vinegar
2 tablespoons fresh lemon juice
3 tablespoons honey
dash nutmeg
dash cloves
¼ teaspoon freshly ground black
 pepper

Bacon adds a lovely smoked flavor to this sweet and sour threesome of red cabbage, onions, and apples simmered in apple cider.

In a large, heavy skillet cook the bacon until crisp. Drain and reserve. Discard all but 1 tablespoon of the drippings. Sauté the onion until tender crisp. Stir in the cabbage, apples, and cider. Cover and simmer for 20 minutes, stirring occasionally. Whisk together the vinegar, lemon juice, honey, nutmeg, cloves, and pepper. Stir into the cabbage mixture. Cover and simmer until the cabbage is tender crisp. Serve hot.

WISP-OF-GARLIC FRIED POTATOES

PREPARATION: 5 MINUTES
COOKING: 10–12 MINUTES
YIELD: 4 SERVINGS

2 tablespoons butter
2 tablespoons olive or vegetable oil
1 clove garlic, peeled
2 baking potatoes, uncooked, peeled
   and sliced into ¼-inch rounds
salt to taste
freshly ground black pepper to taste
2 tablespoons chopped fresh parsley

Just a promise of garlic lifts these fried potatoes out of the ordinary. Garlic lovers are at liberty to improvise.

In a large, heavy skillet melt the butter with the oil over medium heat. Add the garlic clove and stir until just golden. Do not brown. Remove the clove and discard. Sauté the potato slices until tender and golden crisp. Turn often. Do not crowd, to ensure crispness. Sprinkle with salt and pepper and parsley and serve immediately.

SAVORY TOMATO-ONION BROIL

PREPARATION: 5 MINUTES
BROILING: 3–4 MINUTES
YIELD: 6 SERVINGS

3 large, ripe tomatoes, halved
2 tablespoons butter, softened
½ teaspoon Colman's dry mustard,
   dissolved in cold water to paste
   consistency
1 sweet onion, sliced into thin rings
2 tablespoons brown sugar
parsley sprigs for garnish

Great on a lazy Sunday morning, served up with a slice of country ham and fluffy scrambled eggs, onion bagels, and the morning paper.

Place the tomato halves, cut-side up, on a broiler pan. Combine the butter and mustard. Brush each half lightly with the mixture. Top each half with several onion rings. Sprinkle with brown sugar. Brush with remaining butter mixture. Broil for 3–4 minutes. Be careful not to scorch the onion rings. Garnish with parsley sprigs and serve immediately.

BABY LIMAS & ONIONS IN BLUE CHEESE SAUCE

PREPARATION: 5 MINUTES
COOKING: 10 MINUTES
YIELD: 4 SERVINGS

Sweet and tender baby limas team up with celery and onion in a divine sauce, for a change-of-pace vegetable dish.

1 package (10 ounces) frozen baby
   lima beans or 2 cups fresh baby
   lima beans
½ cup chopped celery
½ cup chopped onion
1 cup sour cream
¼ cup blue cheese, crumbled
4 slices cooked bacon, crumbled
1 tablespoon chopped fresh parsley

In a large saucepan, cook the lima beans, celery, and onion in 1 cup water until tender crisp, 5–7 minutes. Drain well. Whisk together sour cream and blue cheese. Stir into vegetable mixture until heated through and cheese melts. Do not boil. Add crumbled bacon. Garnish with chopped parsley and serve immediately.

BRAISED LEEKS & TOMATOES

PREPARATION: 10 MINUTES
COOKING: 30 MINUTES
YIELD: 6 SERVINGS

On the Continent, leeks are called "the poor man's asparagus." They're not as cheap or as plentiful here in America, but their mild, sweet flavor makes leeks worth looking for. Prepare them whenever possible and reap the rewards.

8 medium leeks
2 tablespoons butter
2 tablespoons vegetable oil
2 sweet onions, sliced into rings
2 large tomatoes, peeled and chopped
salt and freshly ground pepper to taste
1 cup chicken stock
2 teaspoons chopped fresh dill

Trim the leeks and remove the coarse upper leaves. Slit open lengthwise. Cut off all but 2½ inches of the green leaves and discard. Wash thoroughly to remove sand and grit. Drain and cut crosswise into 3 or 4 pieces. In a large skillet, melt the butter and oil. Sauté the onion rings until tender. Stir in the leeks and chopped tomatoes. Season to taste. Pour the chicken stock over the mixture. Simmer gently until the leeks are tender crisp. Garnish with chopped dill and serve.

ONION-STUFFED CUCUMBER CANOES

PREPARATION: 25 MINUTES
COOKING: 10 MINUTES
YIELD: 6 SERVINGS

3 medium cucumbers, halved
　　lengthwise
¾ cup water
2 tablespoons butter
1 clove garlic, minced
1 cup chopped onion
1 large tomato, chopped
¾ cup cooked rice
2 tablespoons chopped fresh parsley
¼ teaspoon freshly ground black
　　pepper
salt to taste
¼ teaspoon basil, crumbled
1 hard-boiled egg, chopped
½ cup grated Cheddar cheese

Tuck a savory combination of nutritious goodies into cucumber shells and lend a fresh, flavorful accent to any meal.

Remove the seeds from the cucumber. Discard. Scoop out the pulp, leaving a ¼-inch shell. Chop and set aside. Arrange the shells, cut-side down, in a large skillet. Add the water, cover, and simmer for 5 minutes, until tender. Remove, drain, and cool. In a small saucepan, melt the butter and sauté the garlic and onion until tender. Stir in the cucumber pulp, tomato, rice, parsley, pepper, salt to taste, and basil. Mix well. Fold in the chopped egg and one half of the cheese. Spoon into the cucumber shells. Return to the skillet. Sprinkle with the remaining cheese. Cover and cook until heated through and the cheese melts. Add more water to the pan, if needed. Serve immediately.

ONION & POTATO PARISIENNE

PREPARATION: 25 MINUTES
BAKING: 1 HOUR
YIELD: 6–8 SERVINGS

1 clove garlic, peeled and halved
½ cup butter
4 large potatoes, peeled and thinly
   sliced
2 sweet onions, peeled and thinly
   sliced
salt to taste
freshly ground black pepper to taste
1 cup milk
½ cup cream

A crusty golden surface and rich creamy sauce distinguish this sensational gratin—a classic combination of onion and potato slices seasoned with just the merest touch of garlic. Bon Appétit!

Preheat oven to 400°F. Rub the inside of a gratin dish with the cut side of the garlic cloves. Let dry. Heavily butter the inside of the dish. Alternate the potato and onion slices in rows, slightly overlapping. Season to taste and dot with butter. Layer with remaining slices. Fill the dish ⅔ full. Pour enough milk over the mixture to cover half of it. Top the mixture with a layer of cream to cover all the slices. Dot the top with butter. Bake for 15 minutes. Reduce the heat to 350°F and bake for 45 minutes, until the milk is absorbed. The cream will form a golden crust. Serve bubbling hot.

NOTE: For a crunchier topping, scatter buttered breadcrumbs over the gratin before baking.

ENTRÉES

COOKING IS THE SUREST FORM OF FLATTERY I know. When my husband comes home to a favorite meal, he knows he is the object of my affection. When my family, gathered from far and near, sit down to a holiday dinner with all the trimmings, they reaffirm that home is where the heart is. And when friends gather round our table to share a favorite dish and reminisce, they appreciate my need to fuss rather than extend an invitation to dine out. A homecooked meal shared with those you like and love is a memorable event that makes the world seem brighter and the heart feel lighter. When the domestic sea of tranquility sends up storm warnings, what better way to build a bridge over troubled waters than with a favorite rib-sticker for supper. Differences dissipate quickly over a bubbly steak and kidney pie or a sizzling steak smothered in onions and served with love and laughter.

There is a comforting reassurance in doing one's own cooking and knowing that the food contains only that which you decided to put in it. I freely confess that I am not much on convenience foods. To my way of thinking, they are expensive, lack homemade flavor, and deprive one of the satisfaction of creating something special. I need little in the way of urging to bypass the prepackaged, tasteless conformity of frozen dinners and fast foods for the sheer, unadulterated joy of cooking creatively.

Throughout the years I have endeavored to treat family and friends to the native Scotch and English dishes that my ancestors thrived on. Some of this fare is included in this chapter. Other recipes reach to different parts of the globe to lend a continental touch. Meat, fish, chicken, vegetables, cheese, and eggs are cast as star performers with one or more members of the onion family in supporting roles.

Hooray for home cooking! It adds tremendous meaning to our lives.

When I was a youngster, roast chicken for dinner on Saturday night was a ritual. Preparations commenced early in the day when Granny, the personification of Victorian propriety, bustled into the kitchen, proudly surveyed her domain and announced, "To hell with poverty, let's kill a chicken!"

It was the signal that our gardener, Tom, had been anticipating. Off he shuffled in the direction of the chicken coop to select a privileged young hen which he promptly dressed for the auspicious occasion. Our chickens were a pampered lot. Before going on to greater glory in a stew pot or roasting pan, they pecked their way to plump succulence in contentment and disdain.

If you've never plucked a chicken, you have never experienced the wild exhilaration born of tweezing out the very last pin feather. At Granny's insistence, our chickens were always plucked dry. Scalding them in boiling water to loosen the unyielding feathers was unheard of. It adversely affected the chicken's flavor.

It was a memorable meal: tiny new potatoes roasted in drippings to the right degree of crispness, garden fresh peas shucked at the last moment and steamed briefly with fragrant mint, buttery mashed turnips piled high in a huge tureen, the succulent chicken stuffed to capacity with fragrant sage and onion dressing, and a steaming bowl of bread sauce laced with pan drippings. There were no empty places at the dinner table on Saturday nights.

STUFFED ROAST CHICKEN WITH BREAD SAUCE

PREPARATION: 20 MINUTES
BAKING: 18–20 MINUTES/POUND
YIELD: 4–6 SERVINGS

1 4–5-pound roasting chicken
½ lemon
Sage and Onion Stuffing (see next
  page)
3 tablespoons butter, softened
2 teaspoons rosemary, crumbled
1 tablespoon chopped fresh parsley
¼ teaspoon thyme, crumbled
Bread Sauce (see next page)

A tender roast chicken filled to capacity with moist sage and onion stuffing and served with creamy bread sauce is traditional Saturday night fare in England.

Preheat oven to 375°F. Remove and discard any fat from the chicken cavities. Rinse, drain, and dry the chicken well, inside and out. Rub the inside cavity with the lemon half. Season to taste. Spoon the stuffing lightly into the neck and body cavities. Sew or skewer the openings shut. Tie the legs together. Spoon the extra stuffing into a baking dish and cook during the last one half hour of baking. Place the chicken, breast-side up, in a roasting pan. Combine the butter, rosemary, parsley, and thyme. Rub it all over the chicken. Cover loosely with aluminum foil and roast 18–20 minutes per pound. Brush periodically with any remaining butter mixture. Remove the foil during the last half hour of baking to brown the chicken.

Remove the chicken to a heated serving platter. Pour off the drippings and reserve. Add 1 cup of boiling water to the pan to deglaze. Stir to loosen any brown bits and residue. Remove and discard excess fat from the drippings. Mix the drippings with the pan juices. Stir this mixture into the bread sauce. Let the chicken stand for 15 minutes before carving. Spoon the stuffing into a bowl and keep it warm.

SAGE & ONION STUFFING

PREPARATION: 20 MINUTES   ·   BAKING: 40 MINUTES   YIELD: 4–6 SERVINGS

1 pound bulk pork sausage
3 cups finely chopped onion
1 cup finely chopped celery with
  leaves
1 cup chicken stock
4 cups soft wholewheat breadcrumbs
1 teaspoon sage
¼ teaspoon thyme
½ teaspoon rosemary
2 tablespoons chopped fresh parsley
1 egg, beaten
¼ teaspoon freshly ground black
  pepper

In a large, heavy skillet, crumble the pork sausage into small pieces and cook until the pink disappears. Meanwhile, simmer the onion and celery in the chicken stock until tender. Cool. Drain, and discard any fat from the sausage. Stir in a little of the chicken stock to deglaze the pan. Combine the sausage, breadcrumbs, sage, thyme, rosemary, and parsley. Mix the beaten egg and cooled onion mixture. Combine with the pepper, sausage, and breadcrumbs. Toss lightly to mix well. Refrigerate until ready to use. To bake separately, preheat the oven to 325°F and bake for 40 minutes.

BREAD SAUCE

PREPARATION: 5 MINUTES   COOKING: 10–12 MINUTES   YIELD: 2 CUPS

1 small onion, peeled and stuck with
  2 whole cloves
½ bay leaf
2 cups milk
2 cups soft white breadcrumbs
1 tablespoon butter
1 tablespoon cream
dash nutmeg
2 tablespoons snipped fresh chives

Place the onion, bay leaf, and milk in a heavy saucepan. Heat very slowly to just below the boiling point. Remove from the heat and allow the pan to stand for 20 minutes. Discard the onion and bay leaf. Stir in the breadcrumbs. Return to the stove. Cook and stir until the sauce thickens. Add the butter, cream, and nutmeg. Mix well. Transfer to a gravy boat. Sprinkle with the chives. Serve immediately.

BAKED RED SNAPPER WITH SHERRIED ONION STUFFING

PREPARATION: 10 MINUTES
BAKING: 10 MINUTES/POUND
YIELD: 4 SERVINGS

1 red snapper, whole (2½–3 pounds),
   cleaned and gutted
4 tablespoons lemon juice
Sherried Onion Stuffing
¼ cup melted butter
3 tablespoons dry white wine
1 tablespoon chopped fresh parsley
1 lemon, sliced
Scallion Ruffles (page 27)

Never baked a whole fish? Try this recipe. Stuffed with garden delights and baked to perfection in a buttery wine marinade, red snapper is seafood at its finest. One forkful will convince.

Preheat oven to 375°F. Rinse the fish in cold water and pat dry. Sprinkle the cavity with 2 tablespoons lemon juice. Pack loosely with Sherried Onion Stuffing. Skewer or sew up the opening. Combine the butter, wine, parsley, and remaining lemon juice. Brush generously over the fish. Bake in a large, shallow baking dish just until opaque, about 10 minutes per pound. Baste occasionally with the wine mixture. The fish should just begin to flake. Do not overcook. Serve on a large heated platter. Garnish with lemon slices and Scallion Ruffles.

SHERRIED ONION STUFFING

PREPARATION: 10 MINUTES   COOKING: 20–25 MINUTES   YIELD: 4 SERVINGS

½ cup butter
2 cups chopped onion
½ cup finely grated carrots
½ cup chopped fresh mushrooms
1 clove garlic, minced
¼ cup chopped fresh parsley
¼ cup dry sherry
1 tablespoon lemon juice
1 egg, beaten
½ teaspoon rosemary
½ cup dry cracker crumbs

In a large, heavy skillet, melt the butter. Sauté the onions until tender. Add the carrots, mushrooms, garlic, and parsley. Cook 5 minutes longer. Whisk together the sherry, lemon juice, egg, and rosemary. Stir into the onion mixture. Add the cracker crumbs. Mix well. Any extra stuffing can be baked separately at 375°F for 20 minutes before serving.

PORK & ONION PINWHEEL

PREPARATION: 30 MINUTES
BAKING: 50 MINUTES
YIELD: 4–6 SERVINGS

1 pound lean ground pork
½ pound bulk pork sausage
1 clove garlic, crushed
½ teaspoon rosemary
¼ teaspoon freshly ground black
  pepper
1 egg, beaten
1 teaspoon Worcestershire sauce
½ cup fine breadcrumbs
1 tablespoon butter
½ cup chopped onion
½ cup sauerkraut, drained, rinsed
  twice, and snipped
1 tart green apple, peeled, cored, and
  chopped
½ cup ricotta cheese

Surprises galore in this meatloaf production. A fabulous supporting cast includes tangy sauerkraut, golden onions, tart apple morsels, and creamy ricotta cheese. It's bound to draw rave reviews from the critics.

Preheat oven to 350°F. In a large bowl, combine the ground pork, sausage, garlic, rosemary, pepper, egg, Worcestershire sauce, and breadcrumbs. Mix well. Set aside. Cook the onion in butter until tender and golden, 10–15 minutes. Mix with the sauerkraut, apple, and cheese. Reserve. On wax paper, pat the pork mixture into a 10 × 7-inch rectangle. Spread the onion mixture evenly over the meat, leaving a ½-inch border all around. Starting with the narrow end, roll up in jelly-roll fashion. Lift the loaf carefully into a shallow, baking dish. Bake for 50 minutes. Spoon off any excess fat as it accumulates. Serve in slices.

INDIAN LAMB CURRY

PREPARATION: 40 MINUTES
MARINATING: 1 HOUR
COOKING: 1 HOUR
YIELD: 6 SERVINGS

2 pounds lean, boneless lamb, cut into
   1-inch cubes
1 cup plain yogurt
1 teaspoon Hungarian paprika
1 teaspoon ground coriander
½ teaspoon ground cumin
¼ teaspoon cayenne pepper (or to
   taste)
½ teaspoon ground turmeric
2 tablespoons butter
1 tablespoon vegetable oil
2 cups chopped onion
2 cloves garlic, minced
5–6 slices fresh ginger root, sliced
   wafer thin
1 cup chicken stock
1 small lime, sliced
1 small red Italian onion, peeled and
   sliced thin
¼ cup chopped fresh parsley

Indian cuisine offers an exciting kaleidoscope of flavors, colors, and textures. Since memory serves me, I have rejoiced in the wonderful spiciness of lamb curry. Traditionally, it is accompanied by a marvelous assortment of condiments and served over golden rice. Shub-Bhojain (Hindi for "A fine meal!")!

Place the lamb cubes in a large bowl. Combine the yogurt, paprika, coriander, cumin, cayenne pepper, and turmeric. Mix well. Pour over the lamb and toss to coat well. Cover and marinate at room temperature for 1 hour. Stir occasionally. In a large, heavy saucepan, melt the butter with the oil. Cook the onion slowly over low heat until tender and golden, 20–25 minutes. Add the garlic and cook several minutes longer. Do not brown. Stir in the ginger root slices and chicken stock. Spoon in the lamb and marinade. Mix well. Simmer, covered, for 1 hour or until the lamb is tender. Garnish with the lime and red onion slices. Sprinkle with chopped fresh parsley. Serve with any of the condiments in separate bowls.

CONDIMENTS

Chopped peanuts
Crumbled cooked bacon
Sliced bananas
Snipped chives
Chopped avocado
Chopped hard-boiled eggs
Chutney

HAM LOAF ALASKA WITH CUMBERLAND SAUCE

PREPARATION: 15 MINUTES
BAKING: 1 HOUR
YIELD: 6 SERVINGS

2 cups ground smoked ham
½ pound ground lean veal
½ pound ground lean pork
1 cup soft wholewheat breadcrumbs
4 tablespoons grated onion
½ cup finely minced green bell pepper
2 tablespoons chopped fresh parsley
¼ teaspoon freshly ground pepper
2 eggs
½ cup mayonnaise
½ cup apple juice
1 teaspoon dry mustard
1 tablespoon prepared horseradish
½ teaspoon freshly grated nutmeg
Yam Frosting (see next page)
½ cup finely chopped pecans
Cumberland Sauce (see next page)

Golden yam and pecan frosting teams with piquant Cumberland sauce to add a doubly delicious touch to left-over ham. When the urge to make something different comes over you, try this recipe. It's the perfect panacea.

Preheat oven to 350°F. In a large bowl, combine the ham, veal, and pork. Stir in the bread crumbs, onion, green pepper, parsley, and ground pepper. Whisk together the eggs, mayonnaise, apple juice, mustard, horseradish, and nutmeg. Combine with the ham mixture and mix well. Shape into an oval loaf, 10″ × 4″. Place the loaf in a large, shallow baking pan. Bake, uncovered, for 1 hour. Remove from the oven. Drain off and discard the drippings. Spread the yam frosting over the entire loaf. Sprinkle with the pecans. Broil for several minutes until golden brown. Watch constantly to avoid burning. Transfer the frosted loaf carefully to a heated platter. Serve with Cumberland sauce.

YAM FROSTING

PREPARATION: 5 MINUTES
YIELD: 2½–3 CUPS

A terrific topping that broils crisp and golden

3 cups cooked yams or sweet potatoes
2 tablespoons butter
1 tablespoon brown sugar or honey
¼ tablespoon allspice
1–2 tablespoons cream

Mash the potatoes with the butter, brown sugar, allspice, and enough cream to make a good spreading consistency. Whisk until light and fluffy. Spread thickly. Makes 2½–3 cups.

CUMBERLAND SAUCE

PREPARATION: 10 MINUTES
COOKING: 20 MINUTES
YIELD: 2½ CUPS

Generations old, this treasured sauce recipe has traveled with me since I first left Cumberland on the border of Scotland and England where I was born. Truly a classic with its rich, red color and superb flavor, it combines elegantly with ham, poultry, venison, or roast beef. Traditionally Cumberland sauce is served cold, but if you prefer, spoon it straight from the saucepan.

2 oranges
2 lemons
1 cup port wine
1 small shallot, peeled and diced finely
1 cup red currant jelly
½ teaspoon dry mustard
¼ teaspoon ground ginger
dash Worcestershire sauce

Use a zester or swivel-blade vegetable peeler to remove the rind from the oranges and lemons. Make sure that no bitter white pith is removed. Cut the rinds into match stick strips. Place in a small saucepan with the port wine and shallot. Simmer for 5 minutes. Cool and reserve. Squeeze the juices from the oranges and lemons. Combine with the port wine mixture. Stir in the jelly, mustard, ginger, and Worcestershire sauce. Bring to a boil. Cook and stir constantly over low heat for 15 minutes. Remove from the heat and cool. Refrigerate until the sauce thickens.

ONION & SAUSAGE TOADIE

PREPARATION: 45 MINUTES
BAKING: 30 MINUTES
YIELD: 4–6 SERVINGS

3 tablespoons butter
1 tablespoon vegetable oil
2 onions, sliced
1 pound small pork sausages, pricked
  with a fork
½ cup water
1 cup flour
½ teaspoon baking powder
¼ teaspoon freshly ground black
  pepper
1 teaspoon dry mustard
2 eggs, separated
¾ cup milk
½ cup white Cheddar cheese, grated

Golden onion rings and crusty pork sausages nestle under a puffy blanket of Yorkshire pudding. It's our version of an English treat with the enchanting name of Toad-in-the-Hole.

In a large, heavy skillet, melt the butter with the oil. Cook the onions slowly over low heat until tender and golden, 20–25 minutes. Transfer to a well-buttered ovenproof dish with the drippings. In same skillet, combine the sausages and ½ cup water. Cook until the water evaporates and the sausages are browned. Combine with the onions.

Preheat the oven to 400°F. Combine the flour, baking powder, pepper, and mustard. Whisk together the egg yolks, milk, and cheese. Add the flour mixture. Whisk until light and fluffy. Beat the egg whites until stuff. Fold into the batter. Pour over the sausages and onions. Bake for 30 minutes until puffy and golden brown. Serve immediately.

GARDEN PATCH LASAGNA

PREPARATION: 20 MINUTES
BAKING: 20–25 MINUTES
COOKING: 45 MINUTES
YIELD: 8 SERVINGS

2 cups peeled, chopped tomatoes
1 cup tomato sauce
½ cup dry white wine
1 clove garlic, crushed
½ teaspoon oregano
½ teaspoon basil
1 bay leaf
¼ teaspoon freshly ground black
  pepper
1 tablespoon butter
1 tablespoon olive oil
2 cups chopped onions
½ pound mushrooms, cleaned and
  sliced
1 small carrot, finely chopped
1 small green pepper, cored and
  chopped
1 stalk celery, chopped with leaves
½ pound lasagna noodles, cooked al
  dente
1½ cups grated Parmesan
8 ounces mozzarella cheese slices
1 pound ricotta cheese

Vegetarians rejoice! Here's a meatless main dish brimming with good-for-you ingredients like pasta, vegetables, and cheese, hearty enough to satisfy the most demanding appetites.

Preheat oven to 400°F. In a large saucepan, combine the tomatoes, tomato sauce, wine, garlic, oregano, basil, bay leaf, and black pepper. Simmer for 15 minutes. In a large, heavy skillet, melt the butter with the oil. Sauté the onions until tender and golden, 15 minutes. Stir in the mushrooms, carrot, green pepper, and celery. Cook and stir until tender crisp. Transfer into the tomato mixture. Simmer for 15 minutes longer. Spoon a thin layer of sauce over the bottom of a 12″ × 8″ × 2″ baking dish. Arrange a single layer of noodles on the bottom, overlapping slightly. Top with half the Parmesan cheese. Layer with half the mozzarella slices. Top with half the ricotta cheese. Add another layer of noodles, criss-cross fashion. Spread with the remaining Parmesan and ricotta cheese. Add another criss-cross layer of noodles. Spoon the tomato sauce over the noodles. Remove and discard the bay leaf. Top with the remaining mozzarella slices. Bake for 20–25 minutes or until the top is golden and the lasagna is heated through. Let stand for 15 minutes for easier cutting.

SIZZLE-ICIOUS SIRLOIN STEAK MARINATED IN ONIONS

PREPARATION: 10 MINUTES PLUS
   MARINATING TIME
COOKING: TO DESIRED DONENESS
YIELD: 4 SERVINGS

2½–3-pound steak, ½–2 inches thick
cut cloves of garlic
3 large onions, thinly sliced
freshly ground pepper
oil

When you are planning to broil or grill steak, overnight marinating guarantees new dimensions in flavor.

The night before, rub the steak on both sides with the cut cloves of garlic. Sprinkle with freshly ground black pepper and pat it into the steak.

Spread half of the slices on the bottom of a shallow glass baking dish. Sprinkle with more pepper. Place the steak on the onion slices. Spread the remaining onion slices over the top and sides of the meat. Cover completely. Cover the dish tightly and refrigerate until ready to cook.

Remove the steak from the refrigerator about an hour before cooking. Brush on both sides with oil. Reserve the onions. Season steak to taste. Sauté the onions in butter while the steak is cooking. Serve with the steak.

To barbecue, first sear the steak on both sides to retain the juices while cooking. Then grill to desired doneness. To broil, trim excess fat from the steak. Place the broiler 3 inches from the heat and cook 7 minutes a side for rare, 8 minutes a side for medium, and approximately 10 minutes a side for well done.

STEAK AND KIDNEY PIE

PREPARATION: 30 MINUTES
COOKING: 2 HOURS, 25 MINUTES
YIELD: 6–8 SERVINGS

¾ pound lamb or veal kidneys
2 pounds lean sirloin steak
½ cup unbleached, all-purpose flour
¼ teaspoon freshly ground black
   pepper
2 tablespoons butter
2 tablespoons vegetable oil
2 cups coarsely chopped onion
1½ cups beef stock
½ cup dry red wine
1 teaspoon Worcestershire sauce
½ cup tomato sauce
1 bay leaf
¼ teaspoon thyme
¼ teaspoon rosemary
½ pound small button mushrooms,
   washed and trimmed
pastry for one-crust pie
1 egg, beaten

A favorite of kings and commoners alike, this hearty dish exemplifies the best of British cooking. Tender morsels of steak and kidney mingle succulently in a rich onion gravy under a blanket of flaky pastry. It's even better the second time around.

Preheat oven to 375°F. Wash and trim the fat and membranes from the kidneys. Cut into ½-inch cubes. Trim and cut the steak into 1-inch cubes. Combine the flour and pepper in a large plastic bag. Toss the kidney and steak until well coated. Reserve the remaining flour. In a large, heavy skillet, melt the butter with the oil. Sauté the steak and kidney, a small batch at a time, until browned. Set aside.

Add the onions and cook until tender. Combine the beef stock, wine, Worcestershire sauce, tomato sauce, bay leaf, thyme, and rosemary. Pour over the onions and mix well. Return the meat to the pan. Cover and simmer over low heat for 2 hours. Stir occasionally as the mixture thickens. If necessary, add more beef stock and thicken with the reserved flour. Blend the cold stock and flour together before adding. Allow 1½ teaspoons flour for each cup of stock. Remove to an ovenproof casserole dish. Remove and discard the bay leaf. Add the mushrooms. Place a pie bird in the center. Roll out the pastry and cover the casserole dish. Seal and crimp the edges. Do not stretch the pastry, as it will shrink. Make a slit in the center for the pie bird. Glaze the crust with the beaten egg. Bake until the crust is golden, about 25 minutes. Serve immediately.

NOTE: A pie bird is a hollow ceramic funnel in the shape of a bird. It allows steam to escape through the beak while the pie is baking. If you don't have one, use a regular funnel or make a hole the size of a 50-cent piece for the steam to escape. Pricking the crust isn't sufficient for this amount of stock.

STEAK & ONION KABOBS

PREPARATION: 25 MINUTES
MARINATING: 8 HOURS
COOKING: 5–8 MINUTES
YIELD: 6–8 SERVINGS

2 pounds beef chuck steak, cut in
   1½-inch cubes
Zesty Beer Marinade (see next page)
small, 1-inch, silverskin onions,
   unpeeled
large mushroom caps
red and green pepper chunks
uncooked bacon slices
large pimento stuffed olives

Once you've experienced the fun of kabobbing, you'll be a slave forever. Remember that skillful skewery is just a matter of selecting flavors, textures, and colors to complement one another, and choosing a marinade that brings out the best. Allow yourself 8 hours of marinating time for this recipe.

In a glazed ceramic, glass, or stainless steel bowl, combine the steak cubes and the marinade. Toss well to coat the meat. Cover and refrigerate for 8 hours. Stir occasionally.

To kabob, parboil the unpeeled onions until tender crisp. Cool and peel. Blanch the mushroom caps and pepper chunks in boiling water for 30 seconds to prevent splitting. Drain and set aside. Drain the beef cubes and pat dry. Reserve the marinade. Using long, metal skewers, thread the bacon slices roller-coaster fashion in between alternating pieces of steak, onion, mushroom, pepper, and olive. Thread the onions and olives crosswise to prevent the centers from popping out. Grill to desired doneness 4–6 inches above glowing coals. Baste frequently with marinade to keep moist.

ZESTY BEER MARINADE

PREPARATION: 5 MINUTES

YIELD: 1½ CUPS

1 cup (8 ounces) flat regular beer
½ cup vegetable oil
1 teaspoon dry mustard
½ teaspoon ground ginger
2 tablespoons soy sauce
1 tablespoon honey
2 cloves garlic, minced
dash hot sauce (optional)

In a glazed ceramic, glass, or stainless steel bowl, combine the ingredients. Mix well with a wooden spoon.

SIZZLE SECRETS

- Skewer onions from side to side, not end to end, to prevent the centers from popping out.

- Use flat or square skewers (not round) to prevent the foods from revolving.

- Space meats close together for rare; space wide for well done.

- Keep skewered foods moist by basting regularly.

- Put a cork at the end of the skewer to keep foods from sliding off.

- Grease the grill before using to prevent the food from sticking.

- Scour the grill in hot soapy water after each use.

STUFFED ONION PETALS

PREPARATION: 40 MINUTES
BAKING: 30–40 MINUTES
YIELD: 6–8 SERVINGS

3 sweet onions, unpeeled
½ pound very lean ground lamb
1 cup cooked brown rice
½ cup chopped walnuts
2 tablespoons chopped fresh parsley
1 clove garlic, minced
¼ teaspoon freshly ground black
    pepper
2 ripe tomatoes, chopped
½ teaspoon allspice
1 cup tomato purée
½ cup beef stock
½ cup dry red wine
2 tablespoons fresh lemon juice
1 bay leaf

Individual onion layers become edible wrappers for a savory filling of ground lamb, brown rice, and chopped tomatoes. We've topped this sensational combination with a hearty tomato sauce for great eating.

Wash the onions and place in a large saucepan. Cover with water and simmer, covered, for 20 minutes. Remove, drain, and cool. Cut off the top and bottom of each onion. Using a sharp, pointed knife, make a cut from the top to the bottom of each onion JUST TO THE CENTER. Do not cut all the way through. Remove and discard the outer skin and the membrane just underneath it. Gently peel away each layer to use as a shell for the filling. Each onion should yield 4–5 layers. Reserve the onion centers. Arrange each onion layer, hollow-side up, in a large baking dish. **Preheat the oven to 375°F.**

In a large bowl, combine the ground lamb, rice, walnuts, parsley, garlic, and pepper. Mix well. Gently stir in the tomatoes and allspice. Place 2–3 tablespoons of stuffing in each onion cup. Fold the cup around the stuffing to form a roll. Turn seam-side down. Chop the reserved onion centers. Combine with the purée, beef stock, red wine, lemon juice, and bay leaf. Mix well and pour over the onion rolls. Cover the dish with foil. Bake for 30–40 minutes, basting occasionally. Serve immediately.

COQ AU VIN

PREPARATION: OVERNIGHT + 45
   MINUTES
BAKING: 50–60 MINUTES
YIELD: 4 SERVINGS

---

1 3–3½-pound broiler-fryer, cut up,
   skinned
4 slices lean bacon, diced
2 tablespoons butter
12 small, ½-inch, silverskin onions,
   peeled
12 small white mushrooms, cleaned
½ cup chopped scallions with greens
2 small shallots, peeled and minced
2 cloves garlic, minced
1 small leek (white part only),
   chopped
2 tablespoons unbleached flour
¼ teaspoon freshly ground black
   pepper
salt to taste
½ teaspoon thyme
2 tablespoons chopped fresh parsley
1 bay leaf
2 cups Burgundy or dry red wine
2 tablespoons fresh lemon juice
½ cup apple brandy or cognac
12 very small new potatoes
1 cup thinly sliced carrots
parsley sprigs

Chicken in wine—classic French cuisine at its finest. Be forewarned: This is a make-a-day-ahead recipe to give the flavors mingling time. The results are spectacular. Fifty million Frenchmen can't be wrong.

Trim and discard any fat on the chicken. In a large, heavy skillet, sauté the bacon until crisp. Remove, drain, and reserve. Melt the butter in the skillet and brown individual chicken pieces until golden on all sides. Remove to a large bowl. Sauté the onions and mushrooms quickly until golden. Remove to the bowl. Add the scallions, shallots, garlic, and leek to the pan and sauté until tender. Do not brown. Transfer to the bowl using a slotted spoon. Add the flour, pepper, salt to taste, and thyme to the pan. Stir and cook until browned. Combine the parsley, bay leaf, Burgundy, lemon juice, and brandy. Stir into the flour mixture. Bring to a boil, stirring constantly. Remove from the heat. Add the bacon and pour over the chicken and vegetables. Toss gently to coat well. Cool, cover, and refrigerate overnight.

To prepare, **preheat the oven to 350°F.** Remove any fat from the surface of the bowl and discard. Place the chicken pieces, single layer, in a baking dish. Add the potatoes and carrots. Pour the wine and vegetable mixture over them. Bake, covered, for 45 minutes. Remove the cover and bake until the chicken is tender and glazed. Baste regularly. Remove the bay leaf and discard. Serve the chicken on a large, heated platter. Surround with the vegetables. Pour the sauce over and around the mixture. Garnish with parsley sprigs.

SPANISH EGGS & ONIONS

PREPARATION: 10 MINUTES
COOKING: 45–50 MINUTES
YIELD: 4 SERVINGS

1 tablespoon butter
1 tablespoon olive oil
3 cups thinly sliced sweet onions
1 clove garlic, minced
1 cup chopped Chorizo sausage
¼ teaspoon ground cinnamon
¼ teaspoon ground cumin
dash ground allspice
1 cup tomato sauce
2 cups chicken stock
1 teaspoon red wine vinegar
¼ teaspoon freshly ground pepper
1 cup fresh or frozen peas
6 hard-boiled eggs, quartered
12 small new potatoes, boiled in skins
lemon slices
parsley sprigs

The mere thought of this piquant mix of sweet onions, spicy sausage, peas, and eggs bubbling in savory sauce and served over new potatoes makes my mouth water. It's a quick-to-fix dish reminiscent of sunny Spain. Try it!

In a large, heavy skillet, melt the butter with the olive oil. Pan fry the onions slowly over low heat until tender and golden, 20 minutes. Do not brown. Add the garlic and cook several minutes longer. Stir in the Chorizo sausage and cook for 10 minutes longer. Combine the cinnamon, cumin, allspice, tomato sauce, chicken stock, vinegar, and pepper. Blend into the onion mixture. Simmer gently for 15 minutes. Add the peas. Simmer until the sauce begins to thicken. Gently mix in the eggs. Cook until heated through. Serve over the new potatoes. Garnish with lemon slices and parsley sprigs.

FRITTATA SICILIAN

PREPARATION: 35–40 MINUTES
COOKING: 7–10 MINUTES
YIELD: 4 SERVINGS

1 tablespoon olive oil
¼ pound smoked garlic sausage, diced
1 cup cooked diced potatoes
1 small leek, thinly sliced with tender greens
1 small sweet onion, sliced thin
1 clove garlic, minced
¼ cup chopped green pepper
1 cup sliced mushrooms
2 tablespoons butter
2 tablespoons vegetable oil
6 eggs
3 tablespoons milk
salt and freshly ground black pepper to taste
¼ teaspoon basil
½ cup shredded mozzarella cheese

A frittata is a flat, open-face omelet that you can fill chock full of tasty edibles. They're fun to make and a wonderful way to give your creativity free rein. Let your imagination lead the way.

Preheat the broiler and warm a serving platter. In a skillet, heat the olive oil. Sauté the sausage and potatoes until golden brown. Remove and set aside. Stir in the leek, onion, garlic, and green pepper. Cook until tender crisp. Add the mushroom slices. Cook just until the moisture evaporates. Spoon into the reserved sausage mixture. In a separate 10-inch skillet or omelet pan, melt the butter with the vegetable oil. Swirl to coat the sides. Whisk together the eggs, milk, seasonings, and basil. Pour into the skillet. Over medium heat, stir with the flat end of a fork and shake the pan until the frittata is firm on the bottom. When the top is almost set, remove from the heat. Spread with the sausage mixture and sprinkle with the cheese. Slip under the preheated broiler. Broil until the cheese bubbles. Slide onto the warm platter. Do not fold. Cut into wedges and serve immediately.

BREADS & PASTRIES

Open-faced sandwiches are a way of life in Denmark and are devoured for lunch daily by Danes with a passion for variety. Three ingredients are an absolute must: dark bread, sweet butter, and wafer-thin sweet onion rings. The rest of the ingredients number to infinity.

THERE ARE SOME THINGS THAT LIVE ON FOREVER in one's memory. For me it is the warm, sunny kitchen of my childhood, alive with laughter and activity and fragrant with the perfume of simmering soup and baking bread.

In retrospect, I have spent much of my life in kitchens and without regrets. To me the kitchen epitomizes the hub of the home—a place for gathering together, banishing cares, and appeasing hunger with honest, home-cooked fare.

I happily confess that my favorite kitchen activity, second only to switching on the dishwasher, is baking. It is one of cooking's true joys. It not only fills a house with promises of wonderful things to come, it fills one's self with a sense of accomplishment.

My apprenticeship was served in a country kitchen considered primitive by today's standards with its mammoth brick fireplace and capricious cast-iron range. The oven, infamous for its vagaries and eccentricities, demanded and got constant attention once the steady progression of breads, scones, buns, and pies began. The bliss of biting into the chewy goodness of piping hot bread spread with freshly churned butter made the vigilance well worthwhile.

The oven will always be a miracle worker to me—a place where I can pop in a pan of nondescript batter and recover a crusty, fragrant loaf of mouthwatering goodness. The best argument for doing one's own baking, aside from the pleasures and rewards, is that it isn't at all difficult. If the only thing you are lacking to tackle the recipes ahead is confidence, roll up your sleeves and get busy mixing, stirring, and kneading. You will have the steadfast support of each and every member of the onion family to assure success.

CORNISH ONION & APPLE PIE

PREPARATION: 15 MINUTES
BAKING: 50 MINUTES
YIELD: 8 SERVINGS

pastry for two-crust pie
4 tart apples, peeled, cored, and thinly
    sliced
3 potatoes, peeled, thinly sliced
4 onions, peeled, thinly sliced into
    rings
4 hard-boiled eggs, sliced
½ teaspoon mace
½ teaspoon sage
¼ teaspoon freshly ground black
    pepper
salt to taste
2 tablespoons butter
¼ cup water

Like some people's ancestors, this recipe goes back to the days of the Mayflower. Time has not dulled its taste appeal—try it with roasts or fowl. It's a great accompaniment.

Preheat oven to 375°F. Line a pie pan with bottom pastry crust. Layer the pan with apples, potatoes, onions and eggs. Repeat until used up. Mix the mace, sage, pepper, and salt to taste. Sprinkle over the top layer. Dot with butter. Sprinkle the water over the top layer. Place the top crust over the mixture. Trim and crimp the edges to seal. Make several slits in top of crust. Bake for 50 minutes or until crust is golden brown. Cool. Cut into wedges and serve warm.

BEER & ONION RYE RING

PREPARATION: 2½ HOURS
BAKING: 30 MINUTES
YIELD: 1 LOAF

3 cups unbleached, all-purpose flour
1 cup rye flour
½ cup finely chopped onion
1 clove garlic, minced
½ teaspoon salt
2 teaspoons caraway seeds
1 package active dry yeast
   (1 tablespoon)
1 cup flat, dark beer
¼ cup dark molasses
1 tablespoon butter
1½ cups mashed potatoes, at room
   temperature
½ cup coarsely grated Cheddar cheese

Do try this wonderfully different rye loaf—beer adds body and a malt, nutlike flavor. It is a delicious, hearty bread fabulous for sandwiches of all denominations.

Mix the flours. In a large electric-mixer bowl, combine ¾ cup of the flour mixture, the onion, garlic, salt, caraway seeds, and yeast. Heat the beer, molasses, and butter until very warm. Add to the flour and onion mixture. Beat at medium speed for 2 minutes. Add the mashed potatoes and ½ cup of the flour mixture. Beat at high speed for 2 minutes. By hand, stir in enough additional flour mixture to make a soft dough. Turn onto a lightly floured board. Knead for 10 minutes. Place in a greased bowl and turn to grease on all sides. Cover and let rise in a warm, draft-free place until doubled in bulk.

Punch the dough down and divide into 18 pieces. Shape into balls. Arrange the balls in a greased 12-cup fluted tube pan or a 10-inch tube pan. Cover and let rise until doubled, about 1 hour. Sprinkle with the grated cheese. Place the pan in a cold oven. Set the temperature to 375°F. Bake 30 minutes or until the loaf sounds hollow when tapped. Cool before slicing.

ONION 'N BACON CORN MUFFINS

PREPARATION: 35 MINUTES
BAKING: 20 MINUTES
YIELD: 8–12 MUFFINS

6 slices lean bacon
½ cup finely chopped onion
1 cup unbleached, all-purpose flour
2 teaspoons baking powder
½ teaspoon baking soda
1 tablespoon sugar
½ teaspoon salt
1½ cups yellow or white stone-ground
   cornmeal
½ teaspoon dried rosemary
1 egg
1 cup buttermilk
¼ cup melted butter or bacon
   drippings

Stone-ground cornmeal and a preheated cast-iron muffin pan guarantee the success of this crusty creation from the true South.

Preheat oven to 400°F. In a heavy skillet, sauté the bacon until crisp. Drain and crumble. Pour the drippings into a small bowl and reserve. Sauté the onion until tender. Remove and reserve. Using the bacon drippings, grease a heavy muffin pan. Place the pan in the preheated oven until sizzling hot. Meanwhile, in a large bowl, sift the flour, baking powder, soda, sugar, and salt. Stir in the crumbled bacon, onions, cornmeal, and rosemary. Whisk together the egg, buttermilk, and melted butter or bacon drippings. Stir into the dry ingredients just until moistened. Remove the baking pan from the oven carefully. Quickly pour the batter into each cup, filling it ⅔ full. Bake for 20 minutes, or until golden brown and springy to the touch. Serve piping hot.

SCOTCH SCALLION SCONES

PREPARATION: 12 MINUTES
COOKING: 10–12 MINUTES
YIELD: 8 SERVINGS

2¼ cups unbleached, all-purpose flour
2 teaspoons baking powder
¼ teaspoon baking soda
½ teaspoon salt
½ cup butter, chilled
½ cup finely minced scallions with
   greens
½ cup buttermilk
2 eggs, at room temperature, beaten
1 tablespoon honey

My granny's secret for baking melt-in-your-mouth scones: Make them the same way that porcupines make love: very gently! Her griddle, or girdle as it's called in Scotland, cooked them to golden perfection. Remember never to cut scones with a knife. Always pull them apart with your fingers to preserve the tender texture.

Sift together the flour, baking powder, soda, and salt in a large bowl. Using two knives or a pastry blender, cut in the butter until the mixture resembles small peas. Add the scallions and toss to mix. Whisk together the buttermilk, eggs, and honey. Stir into the mixture with a fork just until the dry ingredients are moistened. Turn out onto a floured surface. Dust your hands with flour and gently press the dough together with your fingertips. Remember the porcupines! Pat gently into a ½-inch circle. Using a floured knife, cut into wedges. **Preheat an ungreased griddle or skillet over medium heat.** Reduce the heat to low. Place the wedges on the griddle. Cook for 10–12 minutes, or until the bottoms are golden and the scones begin to rise. Turn and brown on the other side. Cool slightly. Serve with plenty of butter.

VARIATION

OVEN BAKED SCONES. Preheat the oven to 450°F. Proceed as directed for griddle scones. Before cooking, brush each wedge lightly with milk. Place on a greased baking sheet. Bake for 12–15 minutes, or until raised and golden brown.

CHIVEY COTTAGE CHEESE CRESCENTS

PREPARATION: 20 MINUTES
CHILLING: SEVERAL HOURS
BAKING: 20 MINUTES
YIELD: 24 CRESENTS

1 cup cottage cheese
1 cup unbleached, all-purpose flour
½ cup butter, softened
dash salt
¼ cup finely chopped fresh chives
1 egg, beaten
1 egg white, beaten

A creamy cottage cheese and chive filling hides enticingly inside these diminutive taste treats. Serve anytime, anywhere.

Squeeze excess moisture from the cottage cheese through a cheesecloth or sieve. Combine the flour, butter, ½ cup of cottage cheese, and salt with a wooden spoon until well blended. Divide into 3 balls. Wrap, and chill for several hours. Combine the remaining cottage cheese with the chives and beaten egg. Refrigerate until ready to use.

To bake, preheat oven to 375°F. Roll each ball of dough into a 10-inch circle on a lightly floured surface. Cut each circle into 8 wedges. Spoon 1 teaspoon of cheese mixture onto the wide end of each wedge. Starting at the wide end, roll up each wedge. Place on a lightly greased baking sheet. Shape into crescents. Glaze with the beaten egg white. Bake for 20 minutes or until golden. Cool before serving.

ONION PINWHEELS

PREPARATION: 35 MINUTES
BAKING: 20 MINUTES
YIELD: 8 SERVINGS

1 tablespoon butter
1 tablespoon vegetable oil
1½ cups finely chopped onion
2 tablespoons chopped fresh parsley
dash cayenne pepper
2 cups unbleached, all-purpose flour
3 teaspoons baking powder
½ teaspoon salt (optional)
2 teaspoons sugar
1 cup heavy whipping cream
1 egg, beaten
2 teaspoons milk or cream

Heavenly served straight from the oven with a steaming bowl of favorite soup. Whipping cream instead of butter and milk makes quick work of the mixing.

Preheat oven to 425°F. In a large, heavy skillet, melt the butter with the oil. Cook the onions very slowly over low heat until golden and tender, 20 minutes. Remove, drain, and cool. Combine with the parsley and cayenne pepper. Set aside. Sift the flour, baking powder, salt, and sugar into a large bowl. Add enough cream to make a soft dough. Mix just until the ingredients are dampened. Knead gently 10 times until the dough holds together. On a lightly floured surface, roll the dough into a 8″ × 12″ rectangle. Spread with the onion mixture. Start at the narrow end and roll up carefully in jelly-roll fashion. Using a sharp, wet knife, cut into 8 1-inch slices. Place each slice, flat-side down, on a greased baking sheet. Whisk together the egg and milk. Brush lightly over each slice. Bake for 20 minutes or until golden. Serve immediately.

LEEKS & SAUSAGE IN PUFF PASTRY

PREPARATION: 45 MINUTES
BAKING: 20 MINUTES
YIELD: 8 SERVINGS

1 package (17¼ ounces) frozen puff
   pastry sheets
1 pound lean, bulk pork sausage
2 tablespoons butter
3 leeks, cleaned, trimmed, and sliced
   with some tender greens
2 shallots, peeled and chopped
½ cup cream
¼ cup sour cream

We are inescapably addicted to these divine creations. Tiny ones make elegant appetizers, but for a memorable brunch or lunch, prepare the larger version and indulge.

Preheat oven to 400°F. Thaw the puff pastry. Unfold the sheets. Divide the dough into 8 equal squares with a sharp knife. In a large, heavy skillet, cook the crumbled pork sausage until brown. Remove with a slotted spoon and drain on paper towels. Discard the pan drippings. Melt the butter and sauté the leeks and shallots slowly until tender. Do not brown. Add the cream and cook until it is absorbed. Remove from the heat. Stir in the sausage. Cool slightly. Add the sour cream and mix well. Lightly moisten the edges of the pastry squares with water. Spoon the sausage mixture onto the center of each pastry square, dividing it equally. Fold over one half of each pastry square to form a triangle. Using a fork, press the edges together to seal. Prick the tops in several places. Using a spatula, transfer the turnovers to an ungreased baking sheet. Bake for 20 minutes or until puffy and golden brown. Serve immediately.

OLD-FASHIONED ONION BREAD PUDDING

PREPARATION: 40 MINUTES
BAKING: 40–45 MINUTES
YIELD: 4–6 SERVINGS

1 tablespoon butter
1 tablespoon vegetable oil
1½ cups finely chopped onion
4 slices day-old or stale bread
1 cup milk
¼ cup cream
2 eggs, at room temperature
1 teaspoon Worcestershire sauce
2 tablespoons chopped fresh parsley
salt to taste
¼ teaspoon freshly ground black
   pepper
1 teaspoon toasted sesame seeds

How fondly I recall the bread puddings of my childhood. They were a way of life. Try this one—it's a wondrously delicious way to transform stale bread into an airy, golden delight and brighten up any meal.

Preheat oven to 325°F. In a large, heavy skillet, melt the butter with the oil. Cook the onion slowly over low heat until tender and golden, about 30 minutes. Do not brown. Set aside. Butter a 1½-quart casserole. Butter each bread slice lightly on both sides. Cut into cubes and spread half of them over the bottom of the dish. Sprinkle with the onions. Top with the remaining bread cubes. Whisk together the milk, cream, eggs, Worcestershire sauce, parsley, salt to taste, and pepper. Pour over the bread mixture. Sprinkle with sesame seeds. Bake until the pudding is fluffy and the top crispy golden, about 45–50 minutes.

ONION BAGELS

PREPARATION: 2½ HOURS
BAKING: 20 MINUTES
YIELD: 16 SERVINGS

1 tablespoon vegetable oil
½ cup finely chopped onion
3½–4 cups unbleached, all purpose
   flour
salt to taste
1 package dry yeast (1 tablespoon)
1 cup milk, scalded
½ cup butter, softened
3 tablespoons honey
2 eggs, beaten
1 beaten egg white
minced onion for garnish

BAGELWICHES

There's a new kid on the sandwich block. Split, toasted, and piled high with your favorite makings, such as cheese, corned beef, egg slices, and sweet red onion, bagelwiches are easy, economical, and energizing.

Millions of people start their day with bagels—split, toasted, and slathered with cream cheese. Crusty and shiny on the outside with a moist, chewy interior, these energizing taste delights began with an old Yiddish recipe that advised, "First you take a hole, then put some dough around it!" The water bath reduces the starch and makes for a nice chewy crust.

Heat the oil in a skillet and sauté the onion until tender. Cool. In the large mixing bowl of an electric mixer, combine 1½ cups of flour, the salt, and yeast. Whisk together the hot milk, butter, 2 tablespoons of honey, the eggs, and onions. Gradually add to the dry ingredients. Beat for 2 minutes at medium speed, scraping the bowl occasionally. Or beat 200 strokes by hand. Gradually add 2 cups of the flour. Beat at high speed for 2 minutes. Stir in enough of the remaining flour to make a soft dough. Turn out the dough onto a lightly floured board. Knead for 10 minutes until smooth and elastic. Place the dough in a greased bowl. Turn to coat on all sides. Cover and let rise in a warm place until doubled.

Punch down and knead for 30 seconds. Divide the dough into 16 pieces and shape into balls. Flatten each ball slightly and press through the center with your floured index finger to make a hole. Gentle enlarge by twirling to form a bagel. Place the bagels on a lightly floured board, cover, and let rise for 15 minutes. In a large soup kettle, bring 2 quarts of water to a gentle boil. Add 1 tablespoon of honey. Lower 4 bagels, one at a time, into the water. The bagels will sink, then rise. Boil 1 minute on each side. Remove with a slotted spoon. Drain well.

Preheat the oven to 375°F. Place the bagels on a greased baking sheet. Brush with beaten egg white. Sprinkle generously with minced onion. Bake for 20 minutes, or until golden brown and crusty.

CUMBERLAND ONION SHORTCAKE

PREPARATION: 55 MINUTES
BAKING: 55 MINUTES
YIELD: 6–8 SERVINGS

A treasured family recipe that I consider an heirloom. Cumberland, on the border of Scotland and England where I was born, is famous for its majestic Lake District, William Wordsworth, Cumberland Sauce, rum butter, and wonderful onion shortcake. One bite is worth a million words.

2 cups unbleached, all-purpose flour
2 teaspoons baking powder
1 teaspoon sugar
¼ cup grated aged Cheddar cheese
4 tablespoons chilled butter
2 tablespoons chopped fresh parsley
½ cup buttermilk

In a large bowl, combine the flour, baking powder, sugar, and cheese. Using a pastry blender or two knives, cut the butter into the flour. With your fingertips, rub the mixture together until it resembles coarse meal. Stir in the parsley and buttermilk. Blend well for 30 seconds. Turn out onto a lightly floured surface. Knead the dough gently for 30 seconds with your fingertips. Roll out to fit into a 12"× 8"× 2" baking dish. Press firmly up the sides. Trim the edges. Refrigerate to chill.

ONION FILLING

8 slices lean bacon
4 cups coarsely chopped onion
1 cup cottage cheese
½ cup sour cream
4 eggs, at room temperature
¼ teaspoon freshly ground black pepper
¼ teaspoon rosemary
2 tablespoons chopped fresh chives
2 tablespoons chopped fresh parsley
½ teaspoon freshly grated nutmeg
2 large potatoes, peeled and grated
sour cream

Preheat oven to 400°F. In a large, heavy skillet, sauté the bacon until crisp. Drain and crumble. Remove and discard all but 3 tablespoons of the drippings. Cook the chopped onions slowly over low heat until tender and golden, about 30 minutes. Do not brown. Remove with slotted spoon. Cool and combine with the cottage cheese and sour cream. Whisk together the eggs, pepper, rosemary, chives, parsley, and nutmeg. Stir into the onion mixture. Using a kitchen towel, squeeze out any excess moisture from the potatoes. Combine with the onion filling. Spoon the mixture into the crust. Bake for 10 minutes. Reduce the heat to 350°F and bake for 45 minutes longer, or until a knife inserted near the center comes out clean. Allow to stand for 10 minutes before serving. Cut into squares and garnish with sour cream.

WAGONWHEEL QUICHE

PREPARATION: 30 MINUTES
BAKING: 1 HOUR
YIELD: 8 SERVINGS

Pastry for one 9″ pie crust
5 large eggs, room temperature
1 cup buttermilk
½ cup light cream
1 cup grated Swiss cheese
¼ cup grated Cheddar cheese
½ cup finely diced scallions with
    greens
¾ cup finely diced, cooked smoked
    ham
2 tablespoons chopped fresh parsley
¼ teaspoon freshly ground black
    pepper
salt to taste
10 fresh, thin asparagus spears,
    trimmed
2 ripe tomatoes, sliced

Tender morsels of fresh asparagus and scallions lend an aura of spring to this creamy quiche with its delightful wagonwheel motif. Buttermilk, cheese, and smoked ham take the credit for its deliciously different flavor.

Preheat the oven to 400°F. Line a 9-inch quiche pan with the pastry. Trim and flute the edges. Do not prick the bottom or the sides of the crust. Bake the shell for 8 minutes. Remove from the oven and set aside. Reduce the oven temperature to 375°F. Whisk together the eggs, buttermilk, and cream. Stir in the cheese, scallions, ham, parsley, pepper, and salt to taste. Blanch the asparagus in boiling water for 3 minutes. Drain. Cut 4 of the spears into 1-inch lengths. Arrange the cut sections on the bottom of the pastry. Pour the egg mixture over the cut aspargus. Bake for 20 minutes. Remove from the oven. Working quickly, arrange the remaining asparagus spears to form the spokes of a wheel. Place the tomato slices between the spokes. Return to the oven immediately. Bake for 20–30 minutes longer, or until a knife inserted off center comes out clean. Allow the quiche to stand for 10 minutes before serving. Slice into wedges and serve warm.

CHIVE & CHEESE ZUCCHINI BREAD

PREPARATION: 12–15 MINUTES
BAKING: 50 MINUTES
YIELD: 1 LOAF

1 cup unbleached, all-purpose flour
1 cup wholewheat flour
2 teaspoons baking powder
½ teaspoon baking soda
¼ cup chopped fresh chives
½ teaspoon dried oregano, crushed
¼ teaspoon basil, crushed
¼ teaspoon rosemary, crushed
¾ cup grated Cheddar cheese
1 cup grated unpeeled zucchini
2 tablespoons honey
2 eggs, at room temperature
¼ cup vegetable oil
1 tablespoon lemon juice
1 cup puréed pumpkin
1 teaspoon grated lemon rind

Flakes of Cheddar cheese and chopped chives stud this moist and fragrant loaf. It tastes even better the next day if you can find a hiding place secure enough to ensure its longevity.

Preheat oven to 350°F. Combine the flours, baking powder, baking soda, chives, oregano, basil, rosemary, cheese, and zucchini in a large bowl. Whisk together the honey, eggs, oil, lemon juice, pumpkin, and lemon rind. Combine with the dry ingredients. Mix only until moistened. Turn into a greased and floured 8″× 10″loaf pan. Bake for 50 minutes, or until a wooden pick inserted in the center comes out clean. Allow the loaf to cool in the pan for 15 minutes. Turn out onto a wire rack and cool completely. Slice and serve with cream cheese.

LEEK & ONION TART

PREPARATION: 50 MINUTES
BAKING: 45–50 MINUTES
YIELD: 6 SERVINGS

Basic Pastry Recipe for one 10-inch
    crust
8 slices lean bacon, diced
4 cups sweet onion slices, cut wafer
    thin
2 medium leeks, sliced into rings with
    tender greens
6 eggs, room temperature
1 cup cream
¼ cup milk
2 tablespoons chopped fresh parsley
salt to taste
¼ teaspoon freshly ground black
    pepper
¼ teaspoon freshly grated nutmeg

Make this savory custard pie for brunch, lunch, or supper. Brimming with golden sweet onions, leeks, and morsels of crisp bacon, it possesses the ability to transform any meal into a memorable event.

Preheat oven to 375°F. Line a 10-inch pie or quiche pan with the pastry. Trim and flute the edges. Do not prick the bottom or sides of the crust. Bake the shell for 7 minutes. Remove from the oven and set aside. Reduce the heat to 300°F. In a large, heavy skillet, sauté the bacon until almost crisp. Remove and drain on paper towels. Discard all but 3 tablespoons of the drippings. Stir in the onions and cook slowly over low heat for 20 minutes. Do not brown. Add the leeks and cook for 15 minutes longer, stirring constantly. Whisk together the eggs, cream, milk, parsley, salt, pepper, and nutmeg. Combine with the bacon. Spoon the mixture into the pre-baked pastry shell. Do not fill to the top as the filling will puff. Bake for 45–50 minutes or until golden brown and puffy. Allow the tart to stand for 10 minutes. Cut into wedges and serve warm.

PUMPKIN ONION COOKIES

PREPARATION: 20 MINUTES
BAKING: 12–15 MINUTES
YIELD: 48 COOKIES

½ cup finely chopped sweet onion
¼ cup orange juice
2 cups sifted unbleached, all-purpose
  flour
1 teaspoon baking soda
1 teaspoon cinnamon
½ teaspoon nutmeg
¼ teaspoon allspice
½ cup butter
1 cup brown sugar, firmly packed
1 egg
1 cup canned pumpkin
1 teaspoon vanilla
1 cup chopped pecans

I apologize for the lack of a dessert section. However much I tried, I could not come up with a palatable garlic ice cream pie or an onion whipped cream cake. Nor could Charlie, my husband and chief tester, continue to remain objective and unbiased at the prospect of further attempts to onionize desserts. These sweet onion cookies passed the taste test with flying colors. Please try them.

Preheat oven to 350°F. In a small skillet, steam-sauté the onion in the orange juice until tender. Drain and set aside. Discard any remaining juice. Sift the flour with the soda and spices. Reserve. Cream the butter with the sugar and egg until light and fluffy. Add the pumpkin and vanilla. Mix well. Slowly add the dry ingredients. Stir in the onion and nuts until completely mixed. Drop by rounded teaspoonfuls 2 inches apart onto a greased baking sheet. Bake 12–15 minutes, until lightly browned around the edges. Cool on wire racks.

CONDIMENTS

Back in the good old days, putting up nature's bounty for year-round use was a necessity, not a luxury. Nowadays it isn't as essential to do one's own preserving. However, there are those of us who still enjoy getting involved, not so much out of old habits or thrift, but because it is pleasurable to capture the flavors and scents of the seasons. There is a certain satisfaction in filling a shelf with glistening, colorful jars of homemade condiments and setting a selected few aside for gift giving. Admittedly, some of the inspiration to do it oneself stems from those uneasy pangs of wariness that surface regarding the additives and chemical preservatives that abound in commercial products.

Minor miracles are forthcoming when you marry members of the onion family with fruits, vegetables, spices, herbs, and seasonings. The union brings forth delectable, full-bodied chutneys and relishes that add new dimensions to food. Blandness is banished from the table forever and replaced by a whole new world of taste combinations.

Seasoned vinegars are among the easiest condiments to prepare. Mellow each bottle in a sunny spot in your kitchen and then let their subtle flavoring lend a natural, light, and zesty touch to salad making.

Make your meals more memorable with the savory sparkle of spicy, fruited chutneys. A dollop of tangy relish perks up a lot more than hot dogs. The bold flourish of British Pub Onions never goes unnoticed, especially when served alongside hearty sandwiches or on an appetizing platter of assorted cold meats. Homemade mustard reaches out to flavor picnic fare with a whisper or a wallop, depending on how you spread it.

Capturing and preserving summer's bounty at its peak will reward you with prizes to savor long after the long, hot, sunny days are gone. Homemade condiments are well worth the effort.

FLAVORED BUTTERS

Discount calories and treat yourself to the luxury of butter toppings. Lift everyday foods out of the ordinary by dressing them up with one of our delectable spreads. The flavor possibilities are limitless. Use sweet, unsalted butter, please.

BERCY BUTTER Boil ⅔ cup dry white wine with 1 tablespoon finely minced shallots until reduced to 4 tablespoons. Cool. Cream together 4 tablespoons softened butter, 2 tablespoons chopped fresh parsley, and 1 tablespoon fresh lemon juice. Combine with the shallot mixture and serve at room temperature. Serve with broiled meat or fish.

GARLIC BUTTER Mix ½ cup melted butter, 2 crushed cloves garlic, 1 tablespoon chopped fresh parsley, and freshly ground black pepper to taste. Warm for several minutes. Serve with broiled meat or fish. To serve with lobster, add 1 tablespoon fresh lemon juice.

RAVIGOTE BUTTER Process in blender or cream by hand ½ cup butter, 1 tablespoon drained capers, 1 tablespoon finely minced shallots, 1 tablespoon chopped fresh parsley, 1 teaspoon minced fresh tarragon, 1 teaspoon snipped chives, and 1 teaspoon lemon juice. Use in sandwiches or vegetable, meat, or fish dishes.

SHALLOT BUTTER Using a garlic press, crush 4 small shallots. Mix with ½ cup softened butter. Cream well and season to taste. Cover and chill until the flavors mingle. Serve with steaks, chops, fish, or vegetables.

CHIVE BUTTER Cream ½ cup softened butter with 2 tablespoons finely snipped chives. Season to taste. Refrigerate in a small covered crock. Use for sandwiches, vegetables, steak, chops, or fish.

WHIPPED GARLIC BUTTER

PREPARATION: 5 MINUTES
YIELD: 2 CUPS

2 sticks unsalted butter (4 ounces
   each), softened
6 tablespoons light vegetable oil
2 cloves garlic, crushed (or to taste)

No need to praise the virtues of garlic butter. Suffice to say that it lends an epicurean touch to countless dishes and makes wonderful toast.

Whip the butter in a blender or food processor until light and fluffy. Drizzle in the oil, a little at a time, and blend well. Add the crushed garlic and process until mixed thoroughly. Remove the mixture with a spatula. Store in a tightly covered container and refrigerate.

VARIATIONS

WHIPPED GARLIC BUTTER WITH HERBS. Along with the garlic, add 2 teaspoons minced fresh chives, 1 tablespoon chopped fresh parsley, and 1 teaspoon chopped fresh basil. Process until well blended.

ITALIAN WHIPPED GARLIC BUTTER. Make Whipped Garlic Butter. Combine 2 tablespoons grated Parmesan cheese, 1 teaspoon crushed dried basil, and ½ teaspoon crushed dried oregano. Add along with the garlic and process until well blended.

FLAVORED VINEGARS

PREPARATION: 10 MINUTES
YIELD: 1 QUART EACH

Here's a trio of zesty vinegars, each flavored with a different member of the onion family and sun ripened to tangy perfection. All three are wonderful for marinades, salad dressings, sauces, stews, or any recipe calling for vinegar.

SHALLOT VINEGAR

4 cups white wine vinegar
2 shallots, peeled and minced
2 sprigs parsley
6 whole peppercorns
1 bay leaf
1 small scallion, trimmed slightly for
    garnish

Scald a 1-quart bottle and dry completely. In a saucepan, heat the vinegar just to boiling. Remove and cool. Pour the vinegar into the bottle. Add the shallots, parsley, peppercorns, and bay leaf. Cool completely. Seal tightly with a non-metal stopper. Place the bottle in a sunny window for 2 weeks. Shake daily to mingle the flavors. Strain the vinegar into a sterilized wine bottle or glass container. Add the scallion for garnish. Seal with a cork and store in a dark place.

RED ONION VINEGAR

3½ cups red wine vinegar
2 sprigs parsley
2 sprigs fresh dill
1 small red onion, sliced
6 whole peppercorns
1 small celery stalk with leaves,
    trimmed

Scald a 1-quart bottle and dry completely. In a saucepan, heat the vinegar just to boiling. Cool. Pour the vinegar into the bottle. Add the parsley, dill, onion slices, peppercorns, and celery stalk. Cool completely. Seal tightly with a non-metal stopper. Place the bottle in a sunny window for 2 weeks. Shake daily to mingle flavors. Strain the vinegar into a sterilized wine bottle or glass container. Add parsley sprigs for garnish. Seal with a cork and store in a dark place.

GARLIC VINEGAR

3½ cups red wine vinegar
6 cloves garlic, peeled
2 sprigs parsley
1 bay leaf
6 whole peppercorns
1 sprig leafy tarragon
1 small thin leek, trimmed, split, and washed

Scald a 1-quart bottle and dry completely. In a saucepan, heat the vinegar just to boiling. Cool. Pour the vinegar into the quart bottle. Add the garlic cloves, parsley, bay leaf, peppercorns, and tarragon. Trim the leek to fit in the bottle. Cool completely. Seal tightly with a non-metal stopper. Place the bottle in a sunny window for 2 weeks. Shake daily to mingle the flavors. Strain the vinegar into a sterilized wine bottle or glass container. Add a fresh sprig of tarragon for garnish. Seal with a cork and store in a dark place.

KAYMAK

PREPARATION: 5 MINUTES
YIELD: 2 CUPS

1 package (8 ounce) cream cheese, softened
½ cup butter, softened
½ cup feta cheese, at room temperature
2 tablespoons grated onion
1 clove garlic, crushed

Cut large chunks of crusty, dark rye bread and slather on this delectable cheese spread from Yugoslavia for a terrific taste treat.

Blend all the ingredients in a blender or food processor until light and fluffy. Spoon into a jar with a tight cover. Refrigerate to mingle flavors. Serve at room temperature.

HERBAL GLAZING HONEY

PREPARATION: 15 MINUTES
COOKING: 30 MINUTES
STANDING TIME: 1 WEEK
YIELD: 4, ½-PINT JARS

4 sprigs fresh parsley
2 cloves garlic, peeled and sliced
1 bay leaf
½ teaspoon thyme, crushed
4 cups honey

Reach for this marvelous honey the next time you're cooking chicken, Canadian bacon, pork chops, or ham steaks to glaze each piece to perfection. Or serve it with crisp crackers and cream cheese for a delightful snack.

Place the parsley, garlic, bay leaf, and thyme in a small cheesecloth bag. Tie securely. Heat the honey slowly in a heavy saucepan. Add the bag. Cook very slowly over low heat, stirring occasionally, for 30 minutes. Watch carefully as honey boils over easily. Remove the bag and place it in a clean, 1-quart jar or container. Cool the honey and pour into the container. Let stand, covered, at room temperature for 1 week. Remove and discard the cheesecloth bag. Pour the honey into clean, half-pint containers with lids. Seal and label. Makes 4 jars.

BRITISH PUB ONIONS

PREPARATION: 30 MINUTES
COOKING: 40–45 MINUTES
YIELD: 20–25 ONIONS

½ cup dried currants
2 cups port wine
½ cup white vinegar
½ cup brown sugar, firmly packed
dash cayenne pepper
2 pounds small white boiling onions,
    ¾–1½ inches
1 tablespoon butter
2 tablespoons vegetable oil

A great favorite in pubs throughout Great Britain, these tart and sweet onions hearken back to Magna Carta days. Their pungent flavor is great with cold meats, cheese, and sandwiches. Select the plumpest, firmest onions in sight and don't overcook.

In a large, heavy saucepan, combine the currants, wine, vinegar, sugar, and cayenne pepper. Boil rapidly until the mixture is reduced to 1½ cups. Set aside. Cover the unpeeled onions with boiling water for 3 minutes. Drain, cool, and peel. Cut off and discard the root ends. Using a small, sharp knife, make a shallow X in the top of each onion. In a large, heavy skillet, melt the butter with the oil. Cook the onions slowly over low heat until golden. Shake the pan to turn the onions and prevent scorching. Transfer the onions to the wine sauce. Reheat, cover, and simmer until the onions are tender crisp. Do not overcook. Allow the onions to cool in the sauce. Refrigerate until ready to serve. Serve at room temperature.

PEARL ONION & CORN RELISH

PREPARATION: 30 MINUTES
COOKING: 55–60 MINUTES
YIELD: 2½–3 PINTS

1 tablespoon butter
1 tablespoon vegetable oil
2 large Spanish onions, ½ pound each,
 chopped
2 cloves garlic, minced
½ pound small, ½-inch, pearl onions,
 blanched and peeled
2 cups stewed tomatoes
1 tablespoon brown sugar
1 tablespoon honey
½ cup dry white wine
2 tablespoons cider vinegar
2 tablespoons fresh lemon juice
1 cup water
½ cup dried currants
¼ teaspoon fennel seeds, lightly
 crushed
dash cayenne pepper
1 cup cooked corn

Serve this spicy mixture as an accompaniment to charcoaled steaks or chicken. Try it as a vegetable side dish with roast pork. You'll love it!

In a large, heavy, non-corrosive saucepan, melt the butter with the oil. Add the chopped onions, garlic, and pearl onions. Cook and stir over low heat until golden, 15 minutes. Do not brown. Combine the tomatoes, sugar, honey, wine, vinegar, lemon juice, water, currants, fennel, and cayenne pepper. Stir into the onion mixture. Simmer, covered, over low heat until the onions are tender. Stir frequently. Uncover and cook until thick and syrupy, stirring constantly to avoid scorching. Add the corn. Cook and stir 15 minutes longer. Cool. Spoon into clean, half-pint glass containers with tight-fitting lids. Refrigerate. Bring to room temperature before serving.

SWEET & SPICY ONION MUSTARD

PREPARATION: 15 MINUTES
COOKING: 20–25 MINUTES
YIELD: 3½–4 CUPS

½ cup cold water
1 cup dry mustard
1 cup white wine vinegar
1 cup dry white wine
½ cup chopped onion
2 cloves garlic, crushed
1 bay leaf, crumbled
1 tablespoon honey
dash hot sauce
1 teaspoon dry tarragon
6 whole allspice

Making mustard is so simple, and it yields a homemade condiment to be proud of. Spread it on your favorite sandwich with discretion or abandon—it all depends on your taste buds. It's great for gift giving, decorated with a fancy label and a festive ribbon.

Combine the water and mustard. Mix into a paste. Set aside. Combine the vinegar, wine, onion, garlic, bay leaf, honey, hot sauce, tarragon, and allspice in a large, non-corrosive pan. Boil rapidly until reduced by half. Stir with a wooden spoon. Strain the mixture into a double boiler. Stir in the mustard paste. Cook over simmering water until thick, about 10–15 minutes. Cool. Cover and store in the refrigerator. Stir before using.

RHUBARB & RAISIN CHUTNEY

PREPARATION: 15 MINUTES
COOKING: 45 MINUTES
PROCESSING: 10 MINUTES
YIELD: 2 PINTS

4 cups chopped rhubarb stems
2 cups seedless raisins
3 cups chopped onion
1 cup dark brown sugar
½ cup honey
1½ cups red wine vinegar
½ cup orange juice
1 tablespoon grated orange rind
1 teaspoon ground cinnamon
½ teaspoon ground cloves
¼ teaspoon ground allspice

One of the first harbingers of spring in our garden, tender rhubarb stalks quickly find their way into my trusty sauce kettle. To preserve part of the plenty, I simmer them slowly with a marvelous mixture of seasonings to make chutney from this old family recipe. Serve it with pork, chicken, or ham. Never, never use the leaves—they are toxic.

In a large, heavy, stainless or enamel kettle, combine all the ingredients. Bring to a boil, reduce the heat, and simmer, uncovered, over low heat until the mixture thickens. Stir frequently with a wooden spoon. Cool. Pour the chutney into clean, hot, half-pint jars. Seal and process in a water bath for 10 minutes.

BERMUDA BANANA CHUTNEY

PREPARATION: 20 MINUTES
COOKING: 3 HOURS
PROCESSING: 10 MINUTES
YIELD: 2½–3 PINTS

8 large, ripe bananas, peeled and sliced
4 cups finely chopped Bermuda onion
1 cup chopped dates
½ cup seedless raisins
2 large apples, peeled, cored, and
  chopped
2 cups white wine vinegar
1 teaspoon ground cloves
1 teaspoon allspice
½ cup candied ginger, finely chopped
¾ cup molasses
½ cup fresh lemon juice
¼ cup dark rum

I first tasted this wonderful chutney in Bermuda where banana trees grow in velvety green profusion all over the island. Bermuda bananas are tiny and unbelievably sweet. Simmered with Bermuda onions, dates, and raisins, they make this rum-laced chutney a memorable taste experience. Be adventurous—try it!

In a large enamel or stainless steel pan, combine the bananas, onions, dates, raisins, apples, and vinegar. Bring to a boil. Stir in the cloves, allspice, candied ginger, molasses, and lemon juice. Simmer, uncovered, until the mixture thickens, about 3 hours. Stir occasionally with a wooden spoon. Add the rum and mix well. Cool. Spoon the chutney into clean, hot, half-pint jars. Seal and process in a water bath for 10 minutes.

BITTERSWEET ONION MARMALADE

PREPARATION: 20 MINUTES
COOKING: 1¼ HOURS
STANDING: 24 HOURS
PROCESSING: 10 MINUTES
YIELD: 2½–3 PINTS

---

3 thin-skinned oranges
1 thin-skinned lemon
1 thin-skinned grapefruit
1 cup chopped sweet onions
1 cup peeled, chopped apple
¼ cup white wine vinegar
1 cup apple juice
½ teaspoon ground cloves
½ teaspoon ground ginger
2 cups brown sugar
1 cup dark seedless raisins
1 cup chopped walnuts

When sweet onions wend their way into the marmalade jar, most folks raise an eyebrow. We don't recommend it on breakfast toast, but guarantee its exquisite tart and sweet citrus flavor will lend a touch of class to scrambled eggs with bacon, ham, or sausage. And keep it handy to highlight steak, poultry, and fish.

Wash and dry the oranges, lemon, and grapefruit. Using a sharp knife, cut them into ⅛-inch slices. Discard the seeds and end pieces. Divide the orange and lemon slices into quarters. Divide the grapefruit slices into eighths. In a large, heavy, non-corrosive kettle, combine the slices with the onions, apple, vinegar, and apple juice. Simmer, covered, for 35 minutes, until the peel is tender. Stir occasionally with a wooden spoon. Add the cloves, ginger, sugar, and raisins. Cook, uncovered, over low heat for 30 minutes, or until the mixture thickens. Stir regularly. Remove from the heat. Cool and cover. Let stand at room temperature for 24 hours. Reheat to a boil rapidly, stirring constantly to prevent sticking. Add the walnuts and cook several minutes longer. Cool and pour into clean, hot, half-pint jars. Seal and process in a water bath for 10 minutes.

GRANDMA'S OLD-FASHIONED CHILI SAUCE

PREPARATION: 25 MINUTES
COOKING: 3 HOURS
PROCESSING: 10 MINUTES
YIELD: 4–5 PINTS

12 large, ripe tomatoes
2 green bell peppers, cored and
  chopped
2 red peppers, cored and chopped
1 cup chopped celery with leaves
4 cups coarsely chopped onions
1 clove garlic, minced
2 bay leaves
1 cup dark brown sugar, packed
1½ cups cider vinegar
1 teaspoon cinnamon
½ teaspoon ground cloves
½ teaspoon ground ginger
1 teaspoon dry mustard
dash cayenne pepper
¼ teaspoon freshly ground black
  pepper
salt to taste

I remember my mother's chili sauce simmering on the back burner and filling the house with its heady fragrance. Here is her recipe—guaranteed to make nostrils quiver, mouths water, and memories to recall.

Immerse the tomatoes in boiling water for 30 seconds. Plunge into cold water. Slip off the skins. Core and chop the tomatoes. In a large non-corrosive soup kettle, combine the tomatoes, peppers, celery, onion, garlic, bay leaves, brown sugar, and vinegar. Simmer over low heat, stirring occasionally, for 1 hour. Stir in the cinnamon, cloves, ginger, mustard, and cayenne pepper. Continue to simmer over low heat for 2 hours. Stir regularly with wooden spoon to prevent scorching. Add the black pepper and salt to taste. Remove and discard the bay leaves. Cool and ladle into clean, hot, half-pint jars, leaving a ½-inch head space. Seal and process in a water bath for 10 minutes.

SAUCES & SEASONINGS

I'T'S SO SIMPLE to spark the natural flavor of foods with sauces, gravies, and seasonings. There are moments when accents such as these are just the touch needed to complement a roast, rejuvenate yesterday's leftovers, or upgrade an ordinary dish to gourmet class. From my point of view, that's reason enough for any cook to master the basic gravy and sauce-making skills.

When professional chefs reach into their bag of seasoning tricks, chances are they will come up with one of the four classic flavoring mixes we include in this chapter. Mirepoix, Duxelles, Persillade, and Sofrito are really nothing more than onions, shallots, and garlic used in combination with herbs and vegetables to create wonderfully heady seasonings for all sorts of dishes.

The next time you intend to treat yourself, the family, guests, or the entire shebang to the luxury of butter topping, take a few extra minutes to prepare one of the flavored butter recipes for a distinctive taste sensation (page 130). Homemade mayonnaise, with its velvety texture and wholesome flavor, is worth making if only to observe the magical transformation from liquid into a rich creamy sauce. Our mayonnaise recipe is for Aïoli (pronounce it "i-oh-lee"), a robust dressing with a garlicky persuasion you will find difficult to resist. Once you've tried it, you will discover countless ways to serve it. If you are looking for a savory, tomato-rich sauce full-bodied enough to use in casseroles or serve over meats, poultry, noodles, spaghetti, and vegetables, try Marinara Sauce. Its versatility never ceases to amaze. Buttery, shallot-flavored Béarnaise Sauce lends a touch of haute cuisine to any meal, and Soubise Sauce, the answer to an onion lover's prayer, knows no limitations. Just follow your inclinations.

Let your imagination be your guide in the wonderful world of flavoring. Don't hesitate to experiment with favorite herbs and seasonings. It takes so little effort and there are so many rewards.

FLAVORING MIXES— THE CHEF'S SECRET WEAPON

Aromatic onions, shallots, and garlic—chopped or diced and used in combination with herbs and vegetables—constitute the basis for classic flavoring mixes prized by gourmet cooks the world over.

Do not be intimidated by the names. Three are French and one is Spanish; translated they mean that members of the onion family are busily at work helping to make cooking and dining a joyous experience.

MIREPOIX—*a blend of diced vegetables prepared just before using, usually spread on the bottom of a cooking utensil to enrich the food being braised.* Dice and combine 1 carrot, 1 onion, and 1 celery heart with ½ bay leaf, 1 tablespoon chopped fresh parsley, and 1 sprig thyme. Sauté very slowly in 1 tablespoon butter over very low heat for 30 minutes, until the ingredients are tender but not brown. Remove the bay leaf and season to taste.

DUXELLES—*a mixture of finely chopped shallots and mushrooms used in stuffings, gratins, sauces, and gravies.* Finely chop ¼ pound mushrooms. Wring out as much moisture as possible in a kitchen towel. Sauté 3 tablespoons chopped shallot in 1 tablespoon each butter and olive oil, until tender but not brown. Add the mushrooms and cook over medium heat until the liquid disappears. Stir in 2 tablespoons chopped fresh parsley, ¼ teaspoon freshly ground black pepper, 1 tablespoon fresh lemon juice, and a dash of freshly ground nutmeg. Cook several minutes longer. Season to taste.

PERSILLADE—*a mingle of garlic and parsley used to permeate a dish with flavor quickly, often mixed with stuffings or marinades or added to grills or sautés just before serving.*
Use a marble or ceramic mortar and pestle to pound 2 cloves garlic to a purée. Add 4 tablespoons chopped fresh parsley. Mix thoroughly with your fingers.

SOFRITO—*a basic flavoring in Spanish cuisine using a combination of onions, garlic, and tomatoes, often added to vegetable stuffings, gratins, or sauces.* Sauté 1 cup finely chopped onions in 1 tablespoon olive oil until tender but not brown. Peel, seed, and chop 4 ripe tomatoes. Add to the onions along with 1 diced garlic clove. Cook until the mixture reduces to a thick sauce, 20–25 minutes. Season to taste.

SWEET & SOUR SAUCE

PREPARATION: 5 MINUTES
COOKING: 20 MINUTES
YIELD: 2½ CUPS

Spoon lots of this delectable sauce over slices of baked ham or Canadian bacon for a brunch sensation.

1 can (8 ounces) crushed pineapple
1 cup tomato sauce
½ cup brown sugar
¼ cup red wine vinegar
½ cup chopped scallions with greens
¼ cup chopped green bell pepper
2 tablespoons cornstarch
2 tablespoons fresh lemon juice

Drain the pineapple and set aside. Reserve ½ cup juice. Combine the tomato sauce, reserved juice, brown sugar, vinegar, scallions, and green pepper. Cook and stir until boiling. Reduce the heat and simmer, uncovered, for 10 minutes. Combine the cornstarch and lemon juice. Stir into the sauce. Add the pineapple. Continue to cook, stirring constantly, until thickened.

AÏOLI

PREPARATION: 10 MINUTES
YIELD: 1½ CUPS

½ cup olive oil
½ cup vegetable oil
2 egg yolks
1 teaspoon dry mustard
¼ teaspoon freshly ground black
    pepper
1 tablespoon minced shallots
juice of 1 lemon
3 cloves garlic, peeled

Transylvanian peasants believed garlic capable of dispelling evil and fashioned chains from garlic cloves, which they wore around their necks as protection against witches, the evil eye, and Dracula's bloodthirsty fangs.

A golden, garlic mayonnaise from Provence, France, often called Provence Butter. It's a creamy-smooth, garlicky delight with no resemblance at all to anything storebought. When you make this most famous of all garlic sauces, start with the ingredients at room temperature.

Combine the oils in a measuring cup. In a blender or food processor, combine the egg yolks, mustard, pepper, shallots, and lemon juice. Blend until smooth. Using a garlic press, crush the garlic cloves into the mixture. Blend until smooth. With the motor running, slowly drizzle in the oil mixture in a steady stream. Scrape down the sides if needed. Refrigerate in an airtight jar. Serve with fish, cold meats, or vegetables.

VARIATION

SKORDALIA SAUCE. To make this famous Greek garlic sauce, add ⅓ cup ground almonds, ¾ cup mashed potatoes, 1 tablespoon chopped fresh parsley, and 1 tablespoon lemon juice to the Aïoli after it has thickened. Mix well and serve as a dip with vegetables or crisp crackers.

BÉARNAISE SAUCE

PREPARATION: 15 MINUTES
YIELD: 1 CUP

2 tablespoons minced shallots
2 teaspoons minced fresh tarragon
2 teaspoons minced fresh chervil
¼ cup dry white wine
2 tablespoons tarragon vinegar
¼ teaspoon white pepper
dash cayenne pepper
3 egg yolks, beaten
2 tablespoons fresh lemon juice
¾ cup melted butter
2 tablespoons chopped fresh parsley

Delicately flavored with shallots, this French-born sauce is named after Béarn, a beautiful region in the Pyrenees Mountains, where it originated. It's simply grand on broiled red meats or beef tenderloin and makes a delicious complement for fish and eggs.

In a small, heavy saucepan, combine the shallots, tarragon, chervil, wine, vinegar, pepper, and cayenne. Bring to a boil and simmer until reduced by half. Remove from the heat and cool. In the top of a double boiler over hot water, whisk together the egg yolks and lemon juice. Add the shallot mixture and beat briskly with a whisk or portable electric mixture until thickened. Remove from the water and add the butter in a thin stream, beating constantly. Season to taste and serve garnished with fresh parsley.

SOUBISE SAUCE

PREPARATION: 5 MINUTES
COOKING: 30 MINUTES
YIELD: 2½ CUPS

3 tablespoons butter
2 cups chopped onion
¼ cup unbleached, all-purpose flour
¼ teaspoon ground fresh nutmeg
dash freshly ground black pepper
1½ cups chicken stock
½ cup whipping cream
chopped fresh parsley

A rich, white onion sauce with a multitude of uses. It has an affinity for eggs, fish, poultry, vegetables, and onion lovers.

In a large, heavy skillet, melt the butter. Stir in the onion and cook over low heat until tender. Do not brown. Cool and spoon into a blender or food processor. Whirl until puréed. Return to a heavy saucepan and stir in the flour, nutmeg, and pepper. Cook, stirring constantly, for several minutes. Gradually add the chicken stock. Cook and stir until bubbly and thick. Add the cream and heat through. Serve immediately. Garnish with chopped fresh parsley.

AFRICAN PEANUT BUTTER SAUCE

PREPARATION: 5 MINUTES
COOKING: 30 MINUTES
YIELD: 4 CUPS

¼ cup butter
½ cup finely chopped onion
1 clove garlic, crushed
½ cup chunky peanut butter
2 tablespoons unbleached, all-purpose flour
1 can (6 ounces) tomato paste
2 cups chicken stock
2 tablespoons chopped fresh parsley

Treat your taste buds to a new sensation. Serve this great sauce over chicken, sprinkle generously with chopped peanuts, and enjoy!

In a heavy saucepan, melt the butter. Cook the onion and garlic slowly until tender and golden. Do not brown. Stir in the peanut butter. Mix well. Sprinkle the flour over the mixture and stir until combined. Combine the tomato paste with the chicken stock. Gradually add to the onion mixture. Cook, stirring constantly, until thick and smooth. Serve hot, garnished with parsley.

BOURBON BARBECUE SAUCE

PREPARATION: 10 MINUTES
COOKING: 45 MINUTES
YIELD: 2½ CUPS

1 tablespoon butter
1 tablespoon olive oil
2 cups finely chopped onion
2 cloves garlic, crushed
½ cup molasses
1 cup ketchup
¼ cup red wine vinegar
1 teaspoon dry mustard
¼ teaspoon freshly ground black
   pepper
2 tablespoons fresh lemon juice
½ teaspoon grated lemon rind
1 tablespoon soy sauce
1 tablespoon Hungarian paprika
⅓ cup bourbon whisky

There are as many barbecue sauces as there are outdoor chefs. Try this one. It's fabulous, indoors or out, for spicing up foods and licking off fingers. The alcohol in the bourbon cooks away, leaving but a delectable memory.

In a large, heavy saucepan, melt the butter with the oil. Sauté the onions until tender. Add the garlic and cook 2 minutes longer. Combine the molasses, ketchup, vinegar, mustard, pepper, lemon juice, lemon rind, soy sauce, paprika, and bourbon. Stir into the onion mixture. Bring to a boil, reduce heat, and simmer for 30 minutes, stirring occasionally. Cool and refrigerate in a covered container.

MARINARA SAUCE

PREPARATION: 10 MINUTES
COOKING: 3½ HOURS
YIELD: 1 QUART

2 tablespoons butter
2 tablespoons olive oil
3 cups finely chopped onion
3 cloves garlic, minced
1 can (28 ounces) plum tomatoes,
    undrained
½ cup tomato paste
½ cup grated carrot
¼ cup grated Parmesan cheese
1 teaspoon sugar
¼ teaspoon freshly ground black
    pepper
1 teaspoon dried basil
½ teaspoon dried oregano
1 bay leaf
¼ cup chopped fresh parsley
½ cup red wine
2 cups water

Versatile best describes this thick, rich tomato sauce, long-simmered to bring out the flavors of the herbs. For a smoother sauce, cool and purée. Keep on hand always for spaghetti, lasagna, and pizza.

In a large, heavy saucepan, melt the butter with the olive oil. Cook the onions until tender and golden, 20 minutes. Add the garlic, tomatoes, tomato paste, and carrot. Simmer for 10 minutes, stirring occasionally. Add the remaining ingredients and cook very slowly, uncovered, for 3 hours. Remove and discard the bay leaf. Season to taste. Use immediately or cool and refrigerate or freeze.

ONION & MUSHROOM GRAVY

PREPARATION: 5 MINUTES
COOKING: 25 MINUTES
YIELD: 2½–3 CUPS

¼ cup roast drippings, defatted
1 tablespoon butter
1 tablespoon vegetable oil
2 medium onions, sliced
¼ pound chopped mushrooms
¼ cup unbleached, all-purpose flour
2 cups water or beef or chicken stock
¼ teaspoon freshly ground black
   pepper
salt to taste
2 tablespoons chopped fresh parsley

Succulent pan drippings lend a rich flavor and color to this thick, delicious gravy bubbling with golden onions and tender mushrooms.

Drain the drippings from the roasting pan. Degrease and reserve ¼ cup. In a heavy saucepan, melt the butter with the oil. Cook the onions until tender and golden, 10 minutes. Add the mushrooms. Cook until the liquid evaporates. Blend in the flour. Add the reserved drippings. Cook and stir until light brown. Add the water or stock and stir until thickened. Simmer for 5 minutes. Season with pepper and salt to taste. Serve hot, garnished with parsley.

We may live without friends;
We may live without books;
But civilized man cannot live without cooks.

—Edward G. Bulwelytoon

Or onions!

—Anonymous

INDEX

A

Acorn squash, apple 'n onion stuffed, 86
African peanut butter sauce, 147
Aïoli, 145
Allium. *See* Chive(s); Garlic; Leek(s);
    (Onions); Scallion(s); Shallot(s)
Appetizers, 28–41
    baked garlic spread, 39
    brandied cheese & onion spread, 34
    cheddar cheese & shallot tartlets, 36
    cheese & chive party puffs, 35
    chopped chicken liver savory with sweet
        onion, 40
    ham bites diablo, 33
    lobster-filled party puffs, 37
    marinated shrimp & red onion rings, 31
    onion & eggplant, with pine nuts, 32
    onion & parsley wreaths, 29
    pickled onion, 41
    potted cheese & onion spread, 34
    scallion skinny dip, 30
    stuffed mushrooms Sicilian, 38
Apple(s)
    'n onion stuffed acorn squash, 86
    pie, Cornish onion &, 115
    sweet & sour cabbage combo, 90

B

Baby limas & onions in blue cheese sauce, 92
Bacon, corn muffins, onion 'n, 117
Bagels, onion, 123
Baked garlic spread, 39
Baked goods, 114–128. *See also* Bread(s);
    Pastry; Tart
    chivey cottage cheese crescents, 119
    Cornish onion & apple pie, 115
    Cumberland onion shortcake, 124
    onion 'n bacon corn muffins, 117
    onion bagels, 123
    onion pinwheels, 120
    oven baked scones, 118

Baked goods *(continued)*
    pumpkin onion cookies, 128
    Scotch scallion scones, 118
Baked onions, 77
Baked red snapper with sherried onion stuff-
    ing, 99
Banana chutney, Bermuda, 139
Barbecue sauce, bourbon, 148
Barbecued whole onions, 77
Bare bones turkey chowder with chive
    dumplings, 68
Beans
    baby limas & onions in blue cheese sauce, 92
    Brazilian black, in rum, 85
    hoppin' John, 88
    knock-your-socks-off chili, 70
    Portuguese chickpea & sausage soup, 62
Béarnaise sauce, 146
Beef
    knock-your-socks-off chili, 70
    oxtail & onion stew, 60
    Portuguese chickpea & sausage soup, 62
    sizzle-icious sirloin steak marinated in
        onions, 106
    steak and kidney pie, 107
    steak and onion kabobs, 108
    stock, brown, 56
    Yugoslavian goulash, 58
Beer
    batter, French-fried onion rings in, 82
    & onion rye ring, 116
    marinade, zesty, 109
Beet, pickled, onion, & herring salad, 45
Bercy butter, 130
Bermuda banana chutney, 139
Bermuda onion, 2–3, 17
    dressing, 53
    soup, 66
Bittersweet onion marmalade, 140
Black beans in rum, Brazilian, 85
Black-eyed peas, hoppin' John, 88
Blue cheese sauce, baby limas & onions in, 92

Boiled leeks, 79
Boiled onions, 75
Bouillon, 56
Bourbon barbecue sauce, 148
Braised leeks & tomatoes, 92
Brandied cheese & onion spread, 34
Brazilian black beans in rum, 85
Bread(s), 114. *See also* Baked goods
    beer & onion rye ring, 116
    chive & cheese zucchini, 126
    pudding, old-fashioned onion, 122
    sauce, 98
British pub onions, 135
Broiled whole onion slices, 78
Broth. *See also* Soup(s)
    garlic, 57
    Scotch, MacGregor with oatmeal dump-
        lings, 72
Brown beef stock, 56
Butters, flavored, 130–131

C

Cabbage
    colcannon, 87
    confetti coleslaw, 43
    sweet & sour, combo, 90
Carrot stuffed onions, 80–81
Charcoal-grilled whole onions, 78–79
Cheddar cheese & shallot tartlets, 36
Cheddared onions, 76
Cheese
    blue, sauce, baby limas & onions in, 92
    brandied, & onion spread, 34
    cheddar, & shallot tartlets, 36
    cheddared onions, 76
    & chive party puffs, 35
    cottage, crescents, chivey, 119
    cream, pastry, 36
    potted, & onion spread, 34
    spread, kaymak, 133
    stuffed onions, 80–81

Cheese (continued)
    zucchini bread, chive &, 126
Cherry chicken salad, 51
Chicken, 96
    cock-a-leekie soup, 61
    coq au vin, 111
    liver, chopped, savory with sweet onion, 40
    salad, cherry, 51
    stock, 55
    stuffed roast, with bread sauce, 97
Chickpea & sausage soup, Portuguese, 62
Chili
    knock-your-socks-off, 70
    sauce, grandma's old-fashioned, 141
Chive(s), 23–24
    butter, 130
    & cheese zucchini bread, 126
    chivey cottage cheese crescents, 119
    dumplings, 69
        bare bones turkey chowder with, 68
    growing, 10–11
    party puffs, cheese &, 35
Chivey cottage cheese crescents, 119
Chopped chicken liver savory with sweet
    onion, 40
Chowder. See Soup(s)
Chutney
    Bermuda banana, 139
    rhubarb & raisin, 138
Cock-a-leekie soup, 61
Coconut milk, 48
Colcannon, 87
Coleslaw, confetti, 43
Condiments, 129–141
    Bermuda banana chutney, 139
    bittersweet onion marmalade, 140
    grandma's old-fashioned chili sauce, 141
    pearl onion & corn relish, 136
    rhubarb & raisin chutney, 138
    sweet & spicy onion mustard, 137
Confetti coleslaw, 43
Cookies, pumpkin onion, 128
Cooking tips, 13–14
Coq au vin, 111
Corn
    muffins, onion 'n bacon, 117
    relish, pearl onion &, 136
    stuffed onions, 80–81
Cornish onion & apple pie, 115

Cottage cheese crescents, chivey, 119
Cream cheese pastry, 36
Cream of onion soup, 67
Creamed onions, 75
Creamy horseradish dressing, 53
Crescents, chivey cottage cheese, 119
Crying, how to avoid, 14–15
Cucumber canoes, onion-stuffed, 93
Cumberland onion shortcake, 124
Cumberland sauce, 103
Curry, Indian lamb, 101

D

Dandelion & watercress salad, spring, 50
Dip, scallion skinny, 30
Dressing
    Bermuda onion, 53
    creamy horseradish, 53
    vinaigrette, 44
Dumplings, 69
    chive, 69
    oatmeal, 73
Duxelles, 143–144

E

Eggplant
    appetizer with pine nuts, onion &, 32
    onion &, casserole with lentils, 84
Eggs
    frittata Sicilian, 113
    leek & onion tart, 127
    poached, Portuguese onion soup oporto
        with, 66
    Spanish, & onions, 112
    wasonwheel quiche, 125
Entrées, 95–113. See also Eggs
    baked red snapper with sherried onion
        stuffing, 99
    coq au vin, 111
    Cornish onion & apple pie, 115
    frittata Sicilian, 113
    garden patch lasagna, 105
    ham loaf Alaska with Cumberland sauce,
        102
    Indian lamb curry, 101
    onion & sausage toadie, 104
    pork & onion pinwheel, 100

Entrées (continued)
    sizzle-icious sirloin steak marinated in
        onions, 106
    Spanish eggs & onions, 112
    steak and kidney pie, 107
    steak and onion kabobs, 108
    stuffed onion petals, 110
    stuffed roast chicken with bread sauce, 97

F

Fish. See also Seafood
    baked red snapper with sherried onion
        stuffing, 99
    chowder, stormy weather, 71
    minted green pea & salmon salad, 52
    pickled beet, onion, & herring salad, 45
    Portuguese potato & sardine salad, 46
    salad, Polynesian marinated, 48
Flavored butters, 130–131
Flavored vinegars, 132–133
Flowers, 9
Freezing onions, 15
French-fried onion rings in beer batter, 82
Frittata Sicilian, 113
Frosting, yam, 103

G

Garden patch lasagna, 105
Garlic, 24–26
    broth, 57
    butter, 130
        whipped, 131
    growing, 11
    olives, 47
    purée, 80
    salts or powders, 25
    sautéed, 79
    sautéing, 13
    spread, baked, 39
    vinegar, 133
    wisp-of-, fried potatoes, 91
Garnishes, 26–27
Glazed onions
    golden honey-, 76
    oven baked, 76–77
Glazing honey, herbal, 134
Golden honey-glazed onions, 76

Grandma's old fashioned chili sauce, 141
Gravy, onion & mushroom, 150
Green pea, minted, & salmon salad, 52

H

Ham
    bites diablo, 33
    loaf Alaska with Cumberland sauce, 102
    stuffed onions, 80–81
Health, onions and, 3–7
Herbal glazing honey, 134
Herbs, for onions, 12
Herring salad, pickled beet, onion, &, 45
Honey, herbal glazing, 134
Honey-glazed onions, golden, 76
Hoppin' John, 88
Horseradish dressing, creamy, 53

I

Indian lamb curry, 101
Italian whipped garlic butter, 131

J

Jamaican pepper pork stew, 59

K

Kabobs, steak and onion, 108
Kaymak, 133
Kidney pie, steak and, 107
Knock-your-socks-off chili, 70

L

Lamb
    curry, Indian, 101
    Scotch broth MacGregor with oatmeal
        dumplings, 72
    stuffed onion petals, 110
Lasagna, garden patch, 105
Leek(s), 21–22
    boiled, 79
    braised, & tomatoes, 92
    cock-a-leekie soup, 61
    growing, 11–12
    & onion tart, 127

Leek(s) (continued)
    & sausage in puff pastry, 121
    sautéed, 79
    sautéing, 13
    steamed-sautéed, 79
    vichyssoise, 65
    Welsh, & tomato salad vinaigrette, 44
Leftovers in onion shells, 81
Lentils, onion & eggplant casserole with, 84
Lima beans, baby, & onions in blue cheese
        sauce, 92
Lithuanian mushroom & yogurt soup, 63
Liver stuffed onions, 80–81
Lobster-filled party puffs, 37
Low-salt cooking, 12

M

Marinade, zesty beer, 109
Marinara sauce, 149
Marinated shrimp & red onion rings, 31
Marmalade, bittersweet onion, 140
Medicine, onions in, 5–7
Minted green pea & salmon salad, 52
Mirepoix, 143
Muffins, onion 'n bacon corn, 117
Mushroom(s)
    duxelles, 143
    gravy, onion &, 150
    stuffed, Sicilian, 38
    & yogurt soup, Lithuanian, 63
Mustard, sweet & spicy onion, 137

N

Nut stuffed onions, 80–81
Nutritive value of onions, 4

O

Oatmeal dumplings, 73
    Scotch broth MacGregor with, 72
Old-fashioned onion bread pudding, 122
Olives, garlic, 47
Onion(s), 15–17, 74–82
    & apple pie, Cornish, 115
    apple 'n, stuffed acorn squash, 86
    baby limas &, in blue cheese sauce, 92
    'n bacon corn muffins, 117

Onion(s) (continued)
    bagels, 123
    baked, 77
    barbecued whole, 77
    Bermuda, 2–3, 17
        dressing, 53
        soup, 66
    boiled, 75
    bread pudding, old-fashioned, 122
    British pub, 135
    broil, savory tomato-, 91
    charcoal-grilled whole, 78–79
    cheddared, 76
    cookies, pumpkin, 128
    creamed, 76
    & eggplant appetizer with pine nuts, 32
    & eggplant casserole with lentils, 84
    filling, 124
    flowers, 9
    freezing, 15
    garnishes, 26–27
    giant, 9
    golden honey-glazed, 76
    gourmet, 19
    growing, 7–12
    for health, 3–7
    herbs for, 12
    & herring salad, pickled beet, 45
    kabobs, steak and, 108
    leftovers and, 81
    marmalade, bittersweet, 140
    in medicine, 5–7
    medley stir fry, 89
    & mushroom gravy, 150
    mustard, sweet & spicy, 137
    nutritive value of, 4
    oven baked glazed, 76–77
    oven-roasted, 77
    pan-fried, 77
    parboiled, 75
    & parsley wreaths, 29
    patch spring soup, 64
    pearl, & corn relish, 136
    petals, stuffed, 110
    pickled, appetizers, 41
    pinwheel, pork &, 100
    pinwheels, 120
    & potato Parisienne, 94
    purée, 78

Onion(s) (continued)
  red
    Italian, 18
    rings, marinated shrimp &, 31
    vinegar, 132
  rings, French-fried, in beer batter, 82
  rye ring, beer &, 116
  salts or powders, 25
  & sausage toadie, 104
  sautéed, 77
  sautéing, 13
  sherried, 76
    stuffing, 99
    stuffing, baked red snapper with, 99
  shopping for, 19–20
  shortcake, Cumberland, 124
  sizzle-icious sirloin steak marinated in, 106
  slices
    broiled whole, 78
    oven-baked, 78
    oven-baked, with sherried cream, 78
    sautéed whole, 78
  soup
    cream of, 67
    Portuguese, oporto with poached eggs,
      66
  Spanish eggs &, 112
  spread
    brandied cheese &, 34
    potted cheese &, 34
  steam-sautéed, 77–78
  steamed, 75
  stew, oxtail &, 60
  stuffed, 80–81
  -stuffed cucumber canoes, 93
  stuffing, sage &, 98
  sweet
    chopped chicken liver savory with, 40
    growing, 9–10
  sweet & sour cabbage combo, 90
  tart, leek &, 127
  varieties, 17–19
  and vegetables, 83
  whole, soup, with puff pastry cap, 67
Oven baked glazed onions, 76–77
Oven baked scones, 118
Oven-baked onion slices, 78
  with sherried cream, 78
Oven-roasted onions, 77

Oxtail & onion stew, 60

P

Pan-fried onions, 77
Parboiled onions, 75
Parsley wreaths, onion and, 29
Pastry. See also Tart, Tartlets
  cheese & chive pastry puffs, 35
  cream cheese, 36
  lobster-filled party puffs, 37
  puff, leek & sausage in, 121
Pea, minted green, & salmon salad, 52
Peanut butter sauce, African, 147
Pearl onion & corn relish, 136
Pepper, pork stew, Jamaican, 59
Pepper rings, stuffed, on romaine, 49
Persillade, 144
Pickled beet, onion, & herring salad, 45
Pickled onion appetizers, 41
Pie, Cornish onion & apple, 115
Pine nuts, onion & eggplant appetizer with, 32
Polynesian marinated fish salad, 48
Pork. See also Ham; Sausage
  & onion pinwheel, 100
  stew, Jamaican pepper, 59
  Yugoslavian goulash, 58
Portuguese chickpea & sausage soup, 62
Portuguese onion soup oporto with poached
  eggs, 66
Portuguese potato & sardine salad, 46
Potato(es)
  colcannon, 87
  fried, wisp-of-garlic, 91
  Parisienne, onion &, 94
  & sardine salad, Portuguese, 46
  vichyssoise, 65
Potted cheese & onion spread, 34
Pub onions, British, 135
Pudding, bread, old-fashioned onion, 122
Puff pastry, leek & sausage in, 121
Pumpkin onion cookies, 128
Purée
  garlic, 80
  onion, 78

Q

Quiche, wagonwheel, 125

R

Raisin chutney, rhubarb &, 138
Ravigote butter, 130
Red onion vinegar, 132
Red snapper, baked, with sherried onion stuff-
  ing, 99
Relish, pearl onion & corn, 136
Rhubarb & raisin chutney, 138
Romaine lettuce, stuffed pepper rings on, 49
Rye ring, beer & onion, 116

S

Sage & onion stuffing, 98
Salad(s), 42–53
  cherry chicken, 51
  confetti coleslaw, 43
  dressing. See Dressing
  minted green pea & salmon, 52
  pickled beet, onion, & herring, 45
  Polynesian marinated fish, 48
  Portuguese potato & sardine, 46
  spring dandelion & watercress, 50
  stuffed pepper rings on romaine, 49
  tipsy shrimp boats, 47
  Welsh leek & tomato, vinaigrette, 44
Salmon, salad, minted green pea &, 52
Salt, 12
Sardine salad, Portuguese potato &, 46
Sataras, 58
Sauce(s), 142–150
  African peanut butter, 147
  aïoli, 145
  béarnaise, 146
  bourbon barbecue, 148
  bread, 98
  chili, grandma's old-fashioned, 141
  Cumberland, 103
  marinara, 149
  onion & mushroom gravy, 150
  skordalia, 145
  soubise, 147
  sweet & sour, 144
Sausage
  leek &, in puff pastry, 121
  soup, Portuguese chickpea &, 62
  Spanish eggs & onions, 112
  stuffed onions, 80–81

Sausage (continued)
    toadie, onion &, 104
Sautéed chopped scallions, 79
Sautéed garlic, 79
Sautéed leeks, 79
Sautéed onions, 77
Sautéed shallots, 79
Sautéed whole onion slices, 78
Sautéed whole scallions, 79
Sautéing, 13, 77
Savory tomato-onion broil, 91
Scallion(s), 20–21
    growing, 11
    ruffles, 27
    sautéed chopped, 79
    sautéed whole, 79
    scones, Scotch, 118
    skinny dip, 30
Scones
    oven baked, 118
    Scotch scallion, 118
Scotch broth MacGregor, oatmeal dump-
        lings, 72
Scotch scallion scones, 118
Seafood. See also Fish
    lobster-filled party puffs, 37
    marinated shrimp & red onion rings, 31
    shrimp stuffed onions, 80–81
    tipsy shrimp boats, 47
Seasoning mixes, 142–144
Shallot(s), 22–23
    butter, 130
    growing, 11
    sautéed, 79
    sautéing, 13
    tartlets, cheddar cheese &, 36
    vinegar, 132
Sherried onion stuffing, 99
    baked red snapper with, 99
Sherried onions, 76
Shopping for onions, 19–20
Shortcake, Cumberland onion, 124
Shrimp
    boats, tipsy, 47
    marinated, & red onion rings, 31
    stuffed onions, 80–81
Sirloin steak marinated in onions, sizzle-
        icious, 106
Sizzle-icious sirloin steak marinated in
        onions, 106
Skordalia sauce, 145

Sofrito, 144
Soubise sauce, 147
Soup(s), 54–57, 61–73. See also Stock
    bare bones turkey chowder with chive
        dumplings, 68
    Bermuda onion, 66
    cock-a-leekie, 61
    cream of onion, 67
    garlic broth, 57
    Lithuanian mushroom & yogurt, 63
    Onion patch spring, 64
    Portuguese chickpea & sausage, 62
    Portuguese onion, oporto with poached
        eggs, 66
    scotch broth MacGregor with oatmeal
        dumplings, 72
    stormy weather fish chowder, 71
    vichyssoise, 65
    whole onion, with puff pastry cap, 67
Sour cream, preventing curdling, 54
Spanish eggs & onions, 112
Spring dandelion & watercress salad, 50
Squash, acorn, apple 'n onion stuffed, 86
Steak
    and kidney pie, 107
    and onion kabobs, 108
    sirloin, marinated in onions, sizzle-icious, 106
Steam-sautéed onions, 77–78
Steamed onions, 75
Steamed-sautéed leeks, 79
Stew(s), 54–55, 58–60
    Jamaican pepper pork, 59
    knock-your-socks-off chili, 70
    oxtail & onion, 60
    Yugoslavian goulash, 58
Stock, 54–55. See also Soup(s)
    brown beef, 56
    chicken, 55
Stormy weather fish chowder, 71
Stuffed mushrooms Sicilian, 38
Stuffed onion petals, 110
Stuffed onions, 80–81
Stuffed pepper rings on romaine, 49
Stuffed roast chicken with bread sauce, 97
Stuffing
    sage & onion, 98
    sherried onion, 99
        baked red snapper with, 99
Sweet & sour cabbage combo, 90

Sweet & sour sauce, 144
Sweet & spicy onion, mustard, 137
Sweet onion(s)
    chopped chicken liver savory with, 40
    growing, 9–10
    varieties, 17–19

T
Tart, leek & onion, 127
Tartlets, cheddar cheese & shallot, 36
Tears, how to avoid, 14–15
Tipsy shrimp boats, 47
Tomato(es)
    braised leeks &, 92
    -onion broil, savory, 91
    salad vinaigrette, Welsh leek &, 44
Turkey, chowder, bare bones, with chive
        dumplings, 68

V
Varieties of onions, 17–19
Veal, Yugoslavian goulash, 58
Vichyssoise, 65
Vinaigrette
    dressing, 44
    Welsh leek & tomato salad, 44
Vinegars, flavored, 132–133

W
Wagonwheel quiche, 125
Watercress salad, spring dandelion &, 50
Welsh leek & tomato salad vinaigrette, 44
Whipped garlic butter, 131
Whole onion soup with puff pastry cap, 67
Wisp-of-garlic fried potatoes, 91

Y
Yam frosting, 103
Yogurt soup, Lithuanian mushroom &, 63
Yugoslavian goulash, 58

Z
Zesty beer marinade, 109
Zucchini bread, chive & cheese, 126